The Economics of Youth Restiveness in the Niger Delta

The Economics of Youth Restiveness in the Niger Delta

Christopher N. Ekong, Ph.D
Ettah B. Essien, Ph.D
&
Kenneth U. Onye

Strategic Book Publishing and Rights Co.

First Published in 2013

Strategic Book Publishing and Rights Co.
12620 FM 1960, Suite A4-507
Houston, TX 77065
www.sbpra.com

ISBN: 978-1-62516-540-4

Dedication

This work is dedicated to the good people of the Niger Delta Region whose lives were innocently taken while struggling for the economic emancipation of the Region.

Foreword

The Niger Delta Region of Nigeria has recently come under intense and careful consideration and discussion internationally. The region's rich natural resource endowments, including oil and gas, had been echoed in all development fora and development discussions in the world. In the front row of discussions about the region, as the authors also indicate, is the sustainable use of the region's resource.

In this text, the authors have taken time off to show an evolving strategy for the development of this strategic partner.

The comprehensive nature and structure of this text is shown in its profound style and deepening. The text introduces its savvies by exploring the general background of the oil and gas resource infrastructure in the country. Taking into perspective a very broad and detailed view of what the sector entails, without even limiting its analysis to the Niger Delta Region, it proceeds to review the totality of the Nigerian economy with particular reference to the stylised facts and the behaviour of the macroeconomic variables of the economy. The text indicates oil and gas sector as the major revenue earner to the Nigerian Federation. It therefore goes to show how the macroeconomic variables behave *vis-à-vis* the oil and gas sector performance.

The national outlook of events is thereafter disaggregated to renew and investigate what happens in the region in which the totality of oil produced in the country is domiciled—the Niger

Delta Region. It is interesting to notice the novel approach the text is taking by deviating from the conventional economic methodology to discuss the history and socio-economics of the Niger Delta Region. It also discusses in detail the resources of the region including both renewable and non-renewable natural resources. This exposition shows how diverse and rich the Niger Delta Region is in terms of resources endowment.

Following the tone the text set in totally understanding the environment she desired to study, it followed up with the reasoning for youth restiveness in the Niger Delta. The root causes of youth restiveness are therefore brought up clearly and distinctively. The text, judging from a practical view of events that led to restiveness in the region, from its analyses, submits that there were some benefits, as derivatives from restiveness: The closing of income inequality gap in the region and improvements in socio-economic statistics were of significant importance to note. The text, however, went on to show the very bad and sorry side of restiveness, which gave room for comparison. Kidnapping, hostage taking, and other crime types that perpetuated the region in the active restive period are recorded and they are mind-blowing. Also, the loss in revenue to the nation has been indicated by the text to be monumental. The cost of restiveness is thus shown by the text to quite outstrip its benefits, thus the need to eradicate restiveness. The text goes to suggest far-reaching and novel ideas and methodologies to eradicate or bring to minimum the spate of restiveness in the Niger Delta Region. It is a book that seeks attention. Attention should be accorded it.

Prof. Akpan H. Ekpo
DG, West African Institute For Financial And
Economic Management (WAIFEM)
CBN Learning Centre, P.M.B 2001,
Satellite Town, Lagos, Nigeria

Acknowledgments

We wish to acknowledge, in great depth, the suffering masses of the Niger Delta people who have weathered the storms of lack in a coarse and very difficult environment to eke life out of almost nothing, notwithstanding the plenty that is daily collected from the deep of its land. Their plight inspired us to do this work. We thank our colleagues in the Department of Economics, University of Uyo, whose constructive reviews of our work yielded this piece. We wish to greatly acknowledge the agencies that afforded the Lead author the opportunity of field research whose report we adopted to strengthen the analytical base of the text. We appreciate our families for their patience and support even as we used their time to do this work. We greatly acknowledge God Almighty from whom we drew our strength for this task.

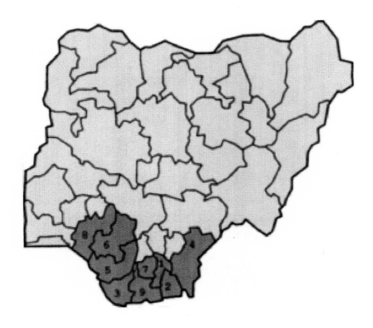

Map of Nigeria numerically showing states typically considered part of the Niger Delta Region: 1. Abia, 2. Akwa Ibom, 3. Bayelsa, 4. Cross River, 5. Delta, 6. Edo, 7.Imo, 8. Ondo, 9. Rivers

ABOUT THE AUTHORS

Christopher N. Ekong, Ph.D
Department of Economics
University of Uyo, Uyo
Nigeria

Ettah B. Essien, Ph.D
Department of Economics
University of Uyo, Uyo
Nigeria

Kenneth U. Onye
Department of Economics
University of Uyo, Uyo
Nigeria

Suggestions for further improvement of the book from fellow teachers and students will be heartily welcomed and can be done through ch_ns_ekong@yahoo.com and/or kennethonye@yahoo.com

Table of Contents

Chapter 1

INTRODUCTION

1.1 Background

The Niger Delta Region of Nigeria constitutes one of the most productive ecosystems in the world. The region is richly blessed with a variety of natural resources and has an abundant array of mineral, water, and forest resources of immense economic potential. This region is noted for remarkable high species diversity, very high rainfall, and a predominantly rainforest vegetation. According to Jones, et al. (1996), the Niger Delta Region of Nigeria is rated as the third largest mangrove forests in the world; with its peculiar geology being the bedrock of enormous mineral deposits that have been the driving force of the Nigerian economy. The Niger Delta Region also extends offshore into the continental shelf of the Atlantic Ocean. The region is approximately 240,000km2 in total area, and most of the oil and gas resources in the region are derived from the continental shelf extension. More importantly, the region sustains Nigeria's number two position on the list of African crude oil producers and the eleventh on the globe.

The Niger Delta Region, through its rich petroleum oil and natural gas deposits, accounts for over 90 percent of Nigeria's foreign exchange earnings and has remained in this position since the early 1970s. Notwithstanding the significant contributions of the region to the wealth of the nation, and the attendant negative impact on its environment as a result of the robust mining and extraction activities in the oil and gas sector in the region, very little or no development impact had been experienced in the region. However, over the years, the numerous cries, agitations, and struggle for the environmental care and economic emancipation of the Niger Delta Region had led to the establishment of several agencies and commissions that were *ab initio* ill-intentioned and thus doomed immediately after takeoff: the 1.5 percent Revenue Commission; the Niger Delta River Basin Development Authority; the Oil Mineral Producing and Development Commission (OMPADEC); and, recently, the Niger Delta Development Commission (NDDC). The realization, even though not well-intentioned, of the central government even to establish these various intervention agencies shows that the government realizes the necessity of some kind of governmental intervention and attention to the development needs of the Niger Delta.

Petroleum exploration began in the first few years of the twentieth century. Organized marketing and distribution started around 1907 by a German company, the Nigeria Bitumen Corporation. In 1914, the Colonial Mineral Ordinance formalized control of oil exploration and the Colonial State, on the basis of the Ordinance, granted concessions exclusively to British and British-allied companies. Under the arrangement, the Anglo-Dutch group Shell D'Archy (later Shell BP) got an oil exploration concession covering the entire 367,000 square miles of Nigeria in 1938. This made Shell dominate the Nigerian oil economy for over six decades. Currently about 50 percent of Nigeria's total production and about 53 percent of its total hydrocarbon reserve base is owned by Shell. In 1956, Shell discovered oil in commercial quantities at Oloibiri in the present Bayelsa State. Shell BP then decided to concede 95 percent of its concessions to other Nigerian companies, leaving itself the prime 16,000 square miles (Luckham, R. and Ibeanu Okechukwu, 2002).

By February 1958, Nigeria had become an oil exporter with a production level of 6,000 barrels per day, although it was not until after the 1967–1970 civil war that it became a major producer on a global scale. A year after Nigeria became an exporter, the federal government sought to take greater control of proceeds of the exports. It therefore passed the 1959 Petroleum Profit Tax Ordinance, which provided for 50/50 profit sharing between the government and producers. This marked the early beginnings of a petro-rentier state (Luckham, R. and Ibeanu Okechukwu, 2002).

Petro-politics in the immediate post-independence period began with the question of distribution of petroleum rents between the federal government and the regional governments. The Binn's Revenue Allocation report recommended that 50 percent be returned to the regions by derivation. In the light of the rapidly rising rents from oil, and based on the Binn's Revenue Allocation formula, it was obvious that there was the potentiality of leaving enormous wealth in the hands of the regional governments, particularly the Eastern regional government, who would get 50 percent derivation from its oil resource. This may explain why that revenue-sharing formula was jettisoned when receipts from oil to the country grew astronomically, while that of other non-oil sector plummeted, as argued further by Luckham an Okechukwu (2002). It is not surprising that oil became a central issue when the Eastern region attempted to secede to form the Independent State of Biafra. Although oil had only a subsidiary role in the outbreak of civil war in Nigeria, it had more direct role in determining the course and outcome of the war. For instance, the decision of Shell BP to pay royalties to the federal government of Nigeria decisively affected the outcome of the war.

Luckham and Okechukwu (2002) also state clearly that oil was also significant in the politics of the war in yet another way—namely, the creation of states and re-drawing of ethnic boundaries. On the eve of the civil war, the federal military government led by Yakubu Gowon changed the administration structure of the country from four regions to twelve states, two of these being Rivers and South Eastern. The two states that represented the minorities of the South Eastern Region were actually the ones where all Nigeria's oil deposits resided. With their creation, the dominant Igbo majority of the South Eastern Region lost total claim to the country's oil resources and therefore had to struggle to convince the two excised minorities of the region to join them in the fight to establish a Biafra Federation. They had no success, because of neo-nationalism and some sense of identity, independence, and liberation that the two new states felt as a result of their long-awaited alienation from the stranglehold of the dominant Igbo majority of the Eastern Region.

1.2 Nigeria's Petroleum Oil Resources

As of 1990, Nigeria had 159 total oil fields and 1,481 wells in operation according to Ministry of Petroleum Resources.

4

The most productive region of the nation is the coastal Niger Delta Basin in the Niger Delta Region, which encompasses 78 of the total 159 oil fields. Most of Nigeria's oil fields are small and scattered, and as of 1990, these small unproductive fields accounted for 62.1 percent of all Nigerian production (Ibeanu, 2006).

Nigeria's deepening in petroleum oil production since it struck oil in Oloibiri and the earnings capacity of the oil sector to the Nigerian economy had made the country to nearly abandon all other non-oil revenue-earning sources in her economy. This concentration, although very negative to the general wellbeing of the country's economy, had moved Nigeria to be ranked as the eleventh highest producer of crude oil in the world and second in Africa with proven reserve of 22.5 billion barrels (Saipem, 2008).

Much of Nigeria's petroleum is classified as "light" or "sweet," meaning the oil is largely free of sulphur. Nigeria is the largest producer of sweet oil in OPEC. This sweet oil is similar in constitution to petroleum extracted from North Sea. Particularly, this Nigerian "sweet crude" is known as "Bonny light." Names of other Nigerian crudes, all of which are named according to export terminal, are Qua Ibo, Escravos blend, Brass River, Forcados, and Pennington Anfan.

There are six petroleum exportation terminals in the country. While Shell Petroleum Development Company of Nigeria (SPDC) owns two, Mobil Nigeria Unlimited, Chevron, Texaco, and Agip own one each. Shell also owns the Forcados Terminal, which is capable of storing 13 million barrels (2,100,000m^3) of crude oil in conjunction with the nearby Bonny Terminal. Mobil operates primarily out of the Qua Iboe Terminal in Akwa Ibom State, while Chevron owns the Escravos terminal located in Delta State and has a storage capacity of 3.6 million barrels (570,000m³). Agip operates the Brass terminal in Brass that has a storage capacity of 3,558,000 barrels (565,700m³). Texaco operates the Pennington Terminal (Saipem, 2008).

1.3 Offshore Oil and Gas Activities - Deepwater Drilling

According to Saipem (2008), deepwater drilling is mainly the underwater oil drilling that exists 400m or more below the surface of the water. Deepwater drilling expands the possible sources for finding new oil reserves. The introduction of deep water drilling allows 50 percent more oil to be extracted. Accordingly, the amount of oil extracted from Nigeria was expected to expand from 15,000 bbl/d (2,400m²/d) in 2010 due to increased offshore or deepwater oil production activities.

In Nigeria, deepwater drilling for oil is especially attractive to oil companies for the following reasons:

1. The Nigerian government has very little share in these activities, so it is hard for them to place restrictions and regulations on companies.
2. The deepwater extraction plants limit the amount of interruptions in production by local militant attacks, seizures due to civil conflicts, and sabotage (McLean and Williams, 2005)

These conditions clearly indicates the economics of why many oil producing companies in Nigeria are today urgently approaching offshore drilling investments, while abandoning on-shore fields.

1.4 Natural Gas

Natural gas reserves are well over 100 trillion ft^3 (2,800km^2); the gas reserves are three times as substantial as the crude oil reserves. The biggest natural gas initiative is the Nigerian Liquified Natural Gas Company, which is operated jointly by several companies and the government.

There is also a gas pipeline, known as the West African Gas pipeline, which, once complete, will allow for transportation of natural gas to West African countries of Benin, Ghana, Togo, and Cote d'Ivoire. The majority of Nigeria's natural gas is flared off and it is estimated that Nigeria loses 18.2 million USD daily from gas flaring ("Natural Gas," OnlineNigeria.com).

The government of Nigeria is currently engaging oil companies, though with an inferior technical capacity, to stop gas flaring in the country by 2010. The oil companies are on the other hand still insisting with more sophisticated and higher technical capacity, underhanded with blackmail, that Nigeria cannot achieve this feat, at least not in the nearest future, which have been achieved in other countries of the world. The question raised here is why things that are conveniently achievable in other countries of the world especially when it comes to best practices in the corporate world are always difficult to be achieved in Nigeria. Cases of complete "flares out" can be seen in oil-producing countries of Europe, America, Asia, and even most of OPEC member states.

1.4.1 The Liquefied National Gas (LNG) Project

Prior to 1982, Nigeria's huge reserves were flared as associated gas in drilling of crude oil. In 1982, the ten major oil companies operating in the country including Shell, Gulf, Mobil, Agip, and Texaco flared about 13.4 billion cubic meters of gas representing 92 percent of all gas produced. In 1997, gas flaring was thought to release 35 million tonnes of CO_2 and 12 million tonnes of methane into the Nigerian atmosphere.

On the economic side, the quantity of gas flared in 1982 was approximately the equivalent of 280,000 barrels of crude oil per day. That would have shored the declining revenues from crude oil export by 25 percent. These considerations led to the establishment of the Nigeria Liquefied Natural Gas (NLNG) project in the Niger Delta Region, which started production in late 1999. The project entails the purchase of natural gas from producers by the NLNG. The company then transports it over 200km of dedicated pipelines into a plant at Finima on the Bonny Island. There, the gas is processed into liquefied natural gas and exported. The project is a joint venture between NNPC (49 percent), Shell (25.6 percent), Elf (15 percent), and Agip (10.4).

1.5 Downstream

Nigeria's total petroleum refining capacity is 445 million barrels per day (70,700m³/d). By 1990, only 240,000 bbl/d (38,000m³/d) was allotted for domestic refining. Subsequently crude oil production for local refineries was reduced further to as little as 75,000 bbl/d (11,900m³/d) in the late 1990s.

The four major refineries in Nigeria include:

1. The Warri Refinery and Petrochemical Plant, which can process 125 million barrels (19,900,000m³) of crude per day

2. The new Port Harcourt Refinery that can produce 150 million barrels per day (24,000,000m³/d)
3. The "old" Port Harcourt and Warri Refinery with negligible production
4. The defunct Kaduna Refinery
5. The Port Harcourt and Warri Refineries both operate at only 30 percent capacity (NigeriaBusinessInfo.com, 2008)

It is therefore estimated that demand and consumption of petroleum in Nigeria grows at a rate of 12.8 percent annually (NigeriaBusinessInfo.com). However, petroleum products are unavailable to most Nigerians and are quite costly, because almost all of the oil extracted by the multinational oil companies is refined overseas, while only a limited quantity is supplied to Nigerians themselves.

1.6 Joint Venture Operations

Joint venture operations entail a shareholding arrangement between the Nigerian National Petroleum Corporation (NNPC) and one or more companies. The joint venture is usually under an operator, while NNPC and other companies are shareholders, with NNPC usually holding equity of 60 percent. The operating cost and risks are shared according to shareholding, which means that the Nigerian state is responsible for 60 percent of the operating costs of each venture (cash calls). Presently, there are six principal joint venture operations involving the major the major oil companies and the NNPC that are summarized below. They are Shell Petroleum Development Company (SPDC) of Nigeria, Mobil Producing Nigeria Unlimited, Nigeria Agip Oil Company, Elf Nig. Ltd, and Texaco Overseas (Nigeria) Petroleum Company.

1.6.1 Joint Venture Operation Production-Sharing Contract

1. In this operation, partners share in the cost of petroleum operations. The contract areas for the OPL's are located in the proportion of their equity shareholding, deep offshore or inland basin.

2. Each partner can lift and separately, dispose of its interest share of crude oil production, subject to inclusive of a 10 year exploration period payment (to government) of petroleum profit tax and royalty. The term of the production-sharing Contract (PSC) is for a period of 30 years.

3. One of the partners is designated as the operator of the joint venture. The contractor bears all the cost of exploration and if oil is found, also bears the cost of subsequent development and production operations. If no oil is found, the contractor is not reimbursed for exploration expenses.

4. The operator prepares and proposes programs. Crude oil produced is allocated as follows: tax oil of work and budget of expenditure, for approval by NAPIMS, the major shareholder. This is to offset tax, royalty and concession rentals due to the government. Two oil regimes are therefore set up here—cost oil and profit oil:

    i. Cost Oil—This is for reimbursement to the contractor for capital investment and operating up to certain limits.

ii.   Profit Oil—The balance after deduction of tax oil and cost oil elements will be shared between the contractor and NNPC.

5. The operator has freedom of action in specific matters, and each party can opt for, and carry out sole risk operations.
6. The contractor pays no corporate tax on its profit
7. NNPC reserves the right to become Operator
8. The commercial aspects of the agreement are covered in the Memorandum of Understanding (MOU). The current MOU provides the companies with the following:

i.   A guaranteed minimum profit of $2.30 per barrel after tax and royalties on their equity.
ii.   A reserves addition bonus in any year that a company's addition to oil and condensate ultimate recovery exceed production for that year.

Joint venture companies in Nigeria account for approximately 95 percent of all crude oil output, while local independent companies operating in marginal fields account for the remaining 5 percent (NigerianBusinessInfo.com, 2008).

1. Royal Dutch Shell (British/Dutch)

The company currently known as the Shell Petroleum Development Company (SPDC) accounted for 50 percent of Nigeria's total oil production (899,000bbl/d or 142,900m^3/d) in 1997 from more than eighty oilfields. This joint venture is composed of NNPC (55 percent), Shell (30 percent), TotalfinaElf (10 percent) and Agip (5 percent) and operates largely onshore, on dry land or in mangrove swamp, in the Niger Delta. The company has more than 100 producing oil fields, and a network of more than 6,000 kilometers of pipelines, flowing through 87 flow-stations. SPDC operates 2 coastal oil export terminals: Forcados and Bonny Terminals.

Shell Nigeria on the other hand owns concessions in four companies, including: Shell Petroleum Development Company (SPDC), Shell Nigeria Exploration and Production Company (SNEPCO), Shell Nigeria Gas (SNG), Shell Nigeria Oil Products (SNOP), as well as holding a major stake in Nigeria Liquefied Natural Gas (NLNG). Shell formerly operated alongside British Petroleum as Shell BP, but BP has since sold all of its Nigerian concessions. Most of Shell's operations in Nigeria are conducted through the Shell Petroleum Development Company (SPDC).

2. Chevron (American)

Chevron Nigeria Limited (CNL) is a joint Venture between NNPC (60 percent) and Chevron (40 percent). Chevron has in the past been the second largest crude oil producer in Nigeria (approximately 400,000 bbl/d ($64,000m^3$/d), with fields located in the Warri region, in Western Niger Delta and offshore in shallow water.

3. Exxon-Mobil (American)

Mobil Producing Nigeria Unlimited (MPNU) is a joint venture between the NNPC (60 percent) and Exxon-Mobil (40 percent) that operates in shallow water off Akwa Ibom

State in the Southeastern Delta with average production of 632,000bbl/d (100,500 m³/d) in 1997, making it the second largest producer, as against 543,000pbd in 1996. Mobil also holds a 50 percent interest in a Production Sharing Contract for a deepwater block further offshore. Due to youth restiveness and militant activities in the Niger Delta, especially in the operations area of Shell and Chevron, and Mobil's offshore base leverage, Mobil has recently overtaken Shell in ranking as the largest producer of crude oil in Nigeria.

4. Agip (Italian)

Nigerian Agip Oil Company Limited (NOAC) is joint venture operated by Agip and owned by the NNPC (60 percent), Agip (20 percent). It produces 150,000bbl/d (24,000m³/d) mostly from small onshore fields.

5. Total (French)

Total Petroleum Nigeria Limited (TPNL) a joint venture between NNPC (60 percent) and Elf (now Total). It produced an approximately 125,000 bbl/d (19,900m³/d) during 1997, both on and offshore. Elf and Mobil are in dispute over operational control of an offshore field with a production capacity of 90,000 bbl/d (14,000m³/d).

6. Texaco (now merged with Chevron)

NNPC Texaco-Chevron Joint Venture (formerly Texaco Overseas Petroleum Company of Nigeria Unlimited), a joint venture operated by Texaco and owned by NNPC (60 percent), Texaco (20 percent) and Chevron (20 percent) currently produces about 60,000 bbl/d (9,500 m³/d) from five offshore fields.

1.7 Petro-Rentier Eras

Since the revenue sharing formula recommended by the Binn's Commission was jettisoned, the federal government of Nigeria retained all derivable revenues and shared to the states in a formula that totally incapacitated the states and regions while making the federal government to be so strong, jettisoning also the true principle of fiscal federalism.

With the advent of the Fourth Republic in 1999, political agitations by oil producing states in the Niger Delta gathered serious momentum with eminent personalities like Arc. Victor Attah, the Governor of Akwa Ibom State (1999 – 2007) leading the struggle for the restoration of the Derivation principle for minerals produced in their communities and states.

To further repress the oil states and tame the ability of the oil producing states from being able to make any meaningful efforts to compel the federal government to pay to them a substantial part of oil proceed as derivation, the federal government of Nigeria in 2001 went to the Supreme Court to seek clarification on the ownership of offshore oil resources of the country—which are located off the coast of the Niger Delta. The federal government eventually won the case, and all such oil found off the coast of Nigeria was attributed to the federal government, leaving states like Akwa Ibom and Ondo, whose substantial part of their oil resources were located offshore, with no oil revenue.

The injustice and lack of "human face" of the Supreme Court judgment, made stakeholders in the Nigerian project to bring pressure to bear on the federal government, who thereafter decided to seek political solution to the on-shore/offshore petroleum ownership debacle. The Nigerian National Assembly reacting to its principle of fair judgment and equal treatment of all peoples and nationalities in the Nigerian project in year 2002 decided on a political and amicable settlement of the post Supreme Court judgment crises by ceding some part or portion of the offshore oil components to the adjoining Niger Delta states (the 200 meters Isobath distance offshore Nigeria's coastline was declared for the states, for all crude oil produced therein, while any production outside this limit was reserved for the federal government. More importantly, the On-shore/Off-shore Oil Dichotomy Act was abrogated, and based on this, the 13 percent derivation principle for oil-producing states as enshrined in the 1999 Constitution of the Federal Republic of Nigeria was fully restored in 2002 after the National Assembly Act and accent by President Olusegun Obasanjo.

Chapter 2

OVERVIEW OF THE NIGERIAN ECONOMY

2.1 Background

The federal Republic of Nigeria that has a landmass of 923,768 square kilometers (km2) is made up of 36 states and 774 local government areas, distributed among the six geo-political zones of the country.

It should, however, be noted here that this text will limit its scope to analyzing oil and economic related activities in only the South-South Zone of Nigeria. This zone has six states, comprising: Akwa Ibom, Bayelsa, Cross River, Delta, Edo, and Rivers. To accommodate the political definition of the oil-bearing South-South Zone, here referred to as the Niger Delta Region, peripheral states like Abia, Imo, and Ondo is considered. These states are adjoining states to the South-South states and are also endowed with Crude Oil. These adjoining states are accommodated in the larger political definition of the Niger Delta by the Nigerian government as represented in the law setting up the Niger Delta Development Commission (NDDC).

As of 1998, land use in Nigeria was indicated thus:

1. Arable—30.96 percent;
2. Permanent Crops—2.79 percent

3. Other—66.25 percent (adapted from Energy Information Administration, Country Analysis, Nigeria 2003 and Central Intelligence Agency (CIA) reported in Saipem, 2004 and the World Fact Book, Nigeria 2003).

The report also put the energy consumption in the country thus:

1. Total Energy Consumption - 0.92 quadrillion Btu
2. CO_2 emissions - 23.5 million CO_2 eq

The huge amount of CO_2 emission shows the high level of gas flaring in the country, which, as of 1998, was not fully gathering and harnessing of gas resources, mostly flared by oil producers (data adapted from Energy Information Administration, Country Analyses, Nigeria, 2003 and Central Intelligence Agency (CIA) reported in Saipem, 2004 and the World Facts Book, Nigeria, 2003).

2.2 The Economy

Nigeria attained political independence in 1960 and a republican status in 1963. Prior to and immediately following political independence from Britain, agriculture remained the mainstay of the Nigerian economy. The dominance of agriculture over all other sectors of the economy in earning revenue for the country was witnessed even in the regional competitiveness, where all the regions competed for significance in agricultural production. Arising from this competition, regional governments had to resort to comparative advantage in agricultural production. The

Western Region therefore concentrated in cocoa production, the Eastern Region produced palm oil, and the Northern Region concentrated in groundnut and cotton production. These agricultural products located Nigeria on the world agricultural map as a major stakeholder and major exporter and provided the early ingredients that kick-started the Nigerian economy.

The structure of the Nigerian economy, however, changed gradually following the discovery of oil in commercial quantities in the late 1950s. With new technologies in the World that culminated in increased demand for crude oil, nicknamed the "black gold," the price of crude oil started rising geometrically, leading to serious boom for oil producing countries like Nigeria. This increased oil price was linked to the 1970s Arab-Israeli war. While the major occupation of the people of Nigeria was and is agriculture, oil became the main driver of the economy, accounting for over 80 percent of revenue earnings and over 20 percent of gross domestic product (GDP).

From attaining political independence in 1960 until now, Nigeria can be said to have experienced two major economic episodes: the period from political independence to 1985 and the period from 1986 to today The first episode was the period of an inward-looking economic policy anchored on import substitution industrialization (ISI), while the second episode, which marked a paradigm shift, was based on export-oriented policy. It came with the comprehensive economic reform package that was meant to diversify the economy away from a single commodity export orientation and open it for competition in line with the prevailing new world economic order.

Policy in the first period was orientated towards the establishment and consolidation of domestic industries with emphasis on their protection from foreign competition. The expectation of the government in this policy era was to institute an industrialization policy framework that would in the near future domesticate hitherto import-oriented establishments in the country.

It was strongly opined that if industries from which the country had hitherto imported its goods and services were established in the country, it would reduce the amount of resources spent on import. This would adjust the Balance of Payments (BOP) situation in the country's favour. Also, the reduction in import volume due to Import Substitution Industrialization (ISI), apart from conserving foreign exchange used in payment for import of goods and services, was also expected to free such saved funds for the government to use in generating employment in the domestic economy because when industries are established, opportunities for employment will be created. The underpinning issue therefore in the Import Substitution Industrialization (ISI) programme was to use the copying, adaptation, and domestication of these foreign technology-based industries in the country to engender technology transfer to the country, while creating the base for the birth of a robust technologically driven private sector.

A major plank of this policy was to ensure the creation of employment, development of skills, and managerial know-how among Nigerians and transferring of the requisite technology from the foreign partners, amongst others. Despite these measures, coupled with the huge inflow of foreign exchange from oil wealth especially from the 1970s, it became clear that the inward-looking policy was not achieving the intended goals. In fact, a clearer but gloomy picture emerged in the early 1980s following the world oil glut and subsequent decline of government revenue with near collapse of the economy. The stabilization measures adopted by government in 1982 did not create the desired impact. The austerity measure—a contractionary fiscal and monetary regime adopted by the civilian government of Shehu Shagari—further worsened the system instead of correcting it. Unemployment and inflation were growing in similar directions, in negation of the Phillips Curve postulation. The Discomfort Index was therefore very high. Reasons strongly adduced for the ensuing economic condition included:

1. High level of corruption in the country
2. Over-dependence on imports
3. Undue opening-up of the domestic economy to international trade
4. An almost and complete total divestment from agriculture
5. Fiscal irresponsibility on the part of the then and previous governments

In order to correct the noticeable gaps that led to the failure of the austerity policies, Nigeria adopted the World Bank/ IMF recommended the Structural Adjustment Programme in 1986. This was meant to totally and comprehensively liberalize the economy with the financial sector reform being a key component of the policy shift.

Thus, in 1986, following the downturn of the economy, the Nigerian government initiated series of reform measures that were aimed at bringing about economic growth and stability. The financial sector restructuring from a regime of direct to indirect control and liberalized market system was a major component of the reform agenda. Indeed, reform in the financial system played a major role in the whole policy redirection. For instance, exchange rate deregulation was expected to boost the non-oil exports and attract foreign investment while the relaxation of constraints and granting of licensing to new banks were envisioned to increase competition; interest rate liberalization and the abolition of credit rationing were reckoned to provide incentives for economic agents to increase their rate of savings and investment.

With the fall in crude oil prices in the late 1970s and early 1980s, the economy went into a period of rapid decline. In 1983 the economy came close to a virtual collapse; real per capita income being about 30 percent lower than at the onset of the oil price boom ten years earlier. The subsequent couple of years witnessed political instability, with two coups in nineteen months during 1983-85. Towards the end of the 1980s, the government introduced a number of economic reforms, involving deregulation of the foreign exchange market, abolition of import licenses, and devaluation of the Naira. However, implementation of the new policies was slow, fiscal discipline remained weak, and substantial budget deficits therefore emerged in the early 1990s. In 1993, the government initiated the Nigerian Economic Summit Group, seeking to identify policy measures to reverse the poor economic performance of the country. One outcome of the Summit was the Economic Action Agenda tagged "Vision 2010," which contained a blueprint for private sector-led growth. Central to this Agenda was the deregulation of the economy. However, little of this was implemented by the government; rather, most of the envisaged market-oriented reforms were reversed in favour of protectionist policies under the guise of guided deregulation.

Nigeria returned to civilian democratic administration in 1999 after the botched Second Republic, which collapsed in 1983, culminating in the return of military rule until 1999. The years after the third period of military entrapment (1983–1999) were associated with a certain degree of economic recovery, relaxed exchange controls, and considerable privatization and deregulation policies.

Thus, the petroleum-rich Nigerian economy, long hobbled by political instability, corruption, and poor macroeconomic management, started undergoing substantial economic reform under the new democratic government that ensued from the retreating military dictatorship in 1999. Though the capital-intensive oil sector provided 20 percent of GDP, over 85 percent of foreign exchange earnings, and about 65 percent of budgetary revenues, Nigeria's earlier governments failed to diversify the economy away from overdependence on this single commodity whose price and quantity demanded remained and still remains volatile and internationally determined.

The manufacturing sector's capacity utilization continued to fall from about 75 percent in the 70s to as low as 40.3 percent and 36.1 percent in 1990 and 2000 respectively. It however rose gradually to the highest rate of 56.5 percent in 2003 before falling slowly to 53.3 percent in 2006. As at 2007, it rose marginally to 53.38 percent. The largely subsistence agricultural sector has not kept up with rapid population growth, and Nigeria, once a large net exporter of food, is now suffering from the familiar Dutch disease, and depends on large food imports. The country's economy is struggling to leverage the vast wealth in fossil fuels in order to displace the crushing poverty that affects about 54.4 percent of her population. Economists refer to the coexistence of vast natural resources wealth and extreme poverty in developing countries like Nigeria as the "paradox of plenty" or the "curse of oil" (Sala-i-Martin and Subramanian, 2003). At a time of peak prices, Nigeria's exports of oil and natural gas shows that 80 percent of Nigeria's oil revenues flows to the government, 16 percent cover operational costs and the remaining 4 percent go to investors.

However, the World Bank has estimated that as a result of corruption, 80 percent of oil revenues benefit only 1 percent of the population. In 2005, Nigeria achieved a milestone agreement with the Paris Club of lending nations to eliminate all of its bilateral external debt. Under the agreement, the lenders were to forgive most of the debt, and Nigeria was to pay off the remainder with a portion of its oil revenues. Outside of the oil sector, Nigeria's economy is highly inefficient. Human capital is underdeveloped. Nigeria was ranked 151 out of 177 countries in the United Nations Development Index in 2004, and non-oil-related infrastructure is inadequate.

Nigeria continued to wallow in substantial economic mismanagement and widespread and persistent poverty, perhaps due mainly to prolonged period of military rule in the country. Incidence of poverty rose to 70 percent in 1990 as indicated by the Central Bank of Nigeria (CBN) in Table 2.1. The country has failed to take full advantage of fertile soil that would have regenerated its agricultural potentials, massive oil resources (including oil, gas and condensate), as well as its abundant human resource endowment.

Following democratic elections in 1999, the first in more than 15 years, and with the renewed and intense efforts to restructure the economy, spearheaded by the new civilian government, a homegrown economic programme called

National Economic Empowerment and Development Strategy (NEEDS) was introduced. With anticipated political stability, some signs of economic recovery sprouted, especially from the financial sector of the economy, due to enormous work being done in the various economic reform programmes of the government. Thus, the financial sector was considered the veritable sector on which the government's revival of the economy hinged. Specifically, in 2004, the government put forth a comprehensive and strategic vision for addressing the country's deep-rooted macroeconomic instability and structural bottlenecks based on the NEEDS document.

The NEEDS was the equivalent of a homemade poverty reduction strategy, covering the four-year period of 2004 to 2007. It aimed at making the private sector the engine of growth, through privatisation, deregulation, and liberalisation, accompanied by infrastructure development, especially in electricity and transport. The NEEDS also developed strategies for agriculture, industry, services, oil, gas and solid minerals. Its purpose was also to raise the country's standard of living through a variety of reforms, including macroeconomic stability, transparency, and accountability. The programme had four essential objectives:

1. To redefine the role of government in the economy
2. To create an enabling environment for the private sector
3. To improve the delivery of social services
4. To seek debt reduction from the international community

The NEEDS sets a growth rate target of 6 per cent per annum, led by the real sector especially agriculture and manufacturing sectors, rather than the oil sector.

Detailed information on selected aggregate macroeconomic and social indicators in Nigeria is presented in Table 2.1. As indicated in this table, the growth rate of GDP dropped from 8.2 percent in 1990 to 5.4 percent in 2000, reflecting the turbulent decade of the 1990s. This downward fall of the trend in growth rate continued into the millennial decade as the indicator continued its freefall to 3.5 percent in 2002. However, the growth rate started to pick up again in 2003, when the highest growth rate of 9.6 percent was recorded; this was attributed to growth in the oil sector, which stood at 23.9 percent. Subsequently, the growth rate remained consistently higher than 5 percent until 2007. An important but contrasting observation from Table 2.1 is that the oil sector experienced negative growth of 1.7 percent, 3.7 percent and 5.9 percent respectively from 2005 to 2007. This is, when put side by side, the general rise and sustenance of oil prices (all brands) in the international market at the period. Economic commentators in the country explained this trend as a direct result of the militant and youth restiveness activities in the Niger Delta Region of the country where all the country's oil production is domiciled. The declining economic fortune of the oil sector in this period caused serious shock on the economy that resulted in other negative fortunes due from the trickle-down effect of the slump in oil sector growth on the economy. This was so since the economy was almost totally anchored on the oil sector. Since it was discovered that the activities of the Niger Delta militant youths led to the falling oil growth rate, it became imperative that policies be put in place to eradicate the restive situation of militant youths in the oil-bearing Niger Delta Region in order to correct the obvious restiveness-led reduction in oil production in the country.

Another interesting observation from Table 2.1 is that the non-oil sector growth jumped from 5.2 percent in 2003, to maintain rare and consistently encouraging positive growth rates of 7.8 percent, 8.4 percent, 9.5 percent and 9.2 percent respectively from 2004 to 2007. Of course, sustaining such growth would be healthy for the economy, because it connotes diversification away from oil.

On federal government finances, available data show that the oil sector was the dominant revenue earner for the government. Clearly, oil accounted for more that 70 percent of the total federally collected revenue for the whole period under review. At the peak in 2006, it accounted for a whopping 88.64 percent. However, the non-oil revenue after a sustained decrease from 23.48 percent in 2001 to 11.36 percent in 2006, started to rise again in 2007 to 21.01 percent perhaps due to a fall in oil exploration activities as a result of militant activities in the Niger Delta Region rather than any significant or sustained improvement in the non-oil sector.

The inflation rate in Nigeria has generally been volatile, high and double digit especially in the 1980s and 1990s. This seems to be the scenario depicted by our data. Apart from 1990 and 2000 that recorded low and single digit rates of 7.5 percent and 6.9 percent, the other years, from 2001 to 2005, presented with volatile and double-digit rates. However, the single digit rates return in 2006 and 2007 with inflation rate at 8.4 percent and 5.4 percent respectively.

Table 2.1: Macroeconomic Indicators for Nigeria, 2000–2007

Economic / Social Indicators	1990	2000	2001	2002	2003	2004	2005	2006	2007
GDP Growth (percent)	8.2	5.4	4.6	3.5	9.6	6.6	5.8	5.3	5.7
Oil Sector Growth (percent)	5.6	11.1	5.2	-5.2	23.9	3.3	-1.7	-3.7	-5.9
Non-oil Sector Growth (percent)	8.6	4.4	2.9	4.5	5.2	7.8	8.4	9.5	9.2
Budget Deficit/ GDP	-2.9	-2.3	-4.3	-5.5	-2.8	-2.6	-0.2	0.3	0.7
Ext. Reserves (percent of GDP)	Na	Na	Na	Na	7.7	11.4	24.4	36.5	42.6
Ext. Reserves (Months of Import cover)	Na	13.6	11.3	7.8	7.2	12.2	18.6	23.0	20.9
External Debt /GDP	106.5	64.9	57.3	72.1	61.1	84.5	69.2	7.4	4.0
Manufacturing Capacity Utilization	40.3	36.1	42.7	54.9	56.5	55.7	54.8	53.3	53.38
Oil Revenue (percent of total)	73.28	83.50	76.52	71.07	80.55	85.57	85.85	88.64	78.08

(Continued)

27

Economic / Social Indicators	1990	2000	2001	2002	2003	2004	2005	2006	2007
Non-Oil Revenue (percent of total)	26.72	16.50	23.48	28.93	19.45	14.43	14.15	11.36	21.01
Domestic Debt/ GDP	31.3	32.2	36.6	26.1	28.6	25.3	20.8	18.6	19.2
Overall BOP/GDP	-2.1	6.9	0.5	-10.3	-2.3	5.2	10.5	12.7	1.4
Inflation Rate	7.5	6.9	18.9	12.9	14.0	15.0	17.6	8.4	5.4
Average Official Exch. Rate	7.9	101.7	111.9	121.0	127.8	132.8	132.9	128.5	127.4
Lending Rate	27.7	21.6	21.3	22.5	22.9	20.7	19.2	18.6	18.7
Narrow Money Growth	30.7	28.7	28.1	15.9	13.8	8.6	9.3	20.4	0.6
Broad Money Growth	44.9	48.1	27.0	21.6	16.9	6.5	18.9	29.1	11.0
Population Growth Rate (percent)	2.8	2.8	2.8	2.8	2.8	2.8	2.8	2.8	3.2
Life Expectancy (years)	Na	Na	54.0	54.0	54.0	54.0	54.0	54.0	54.0
Adult Literacy Rate (percent)	na	57	57	57	57.0	62.0	57.0	64.2	64.5
Incidence of Poverty (percent)	70.0	66.0	Na	Na	Na	54.4	54.4	54.4	54.4

Sources: CBN Annual Reports and Statements of Accounts (Various years).

Other economic fundamentals indicate that there was an improved attempt to better manage the economy during the period 2000 to 2007. Budget deficit as a ratio of GDP began to improve between 2005 and 2007 while external reserves could cover about 20 months of imports during the same period. All other economic fundamentals seem to move in the right direction. However, the incidence of poverty remains quite high for a country endowed with enormous human and natural resources.

A longer-term economic development program is the United Nations (UN)-sponsored National Millennium Development Goals (MDGs) for Nigeria. Under the program, which covers the years from 2000 to 2015, Nigeria is committed to achieving a wide range of ambitious objectives involving poverty reduction, education, gender equality, health, the environment, and international development cooperation. In an update released in 2004, the UN found that Nigeria was making progress toward achieving several goals but was falling short on others. Specifically, Nigeria had advanced efforts to provide universal primary education, protect the environment, and develop a global development partnership. However, the country lagged behind on the goals of eliminating extreme poverty and hunger, reducing child and maternal mortality, and combating diseases, such as human immunodeficiency virus/acquired immune deficiency syndrome (HIV/AIDS), and malaria (UNDP, 2004).

Table 2.2 is a further display of economic and social statistics of Nigeria. The table indicates that as of 2008, the percentage of all foreign aids to Nigeria measured as a percentage of the country's GDP was 0.4 percent. This show that aids was not very significant in influencing the economy or causing any serious and noticeable shock and effect if the variable is disturbed. This situation is unlike some developing countries in the world and especially in Africa where aid is a significant proportion of their GDPs. They depend mostly or totally on aids and assistance from the international aid funds.

The Gini Index that shows that the income distribution rate as of the time the data were collated (2005 – 2008) was 43.7 nationally in Nigeria. This can be said to be halfway to equitable income distribution, which is zero. Chapter 8 of this text discusses income distribution more elaborately with an in-depth analysis. Notice that 43.7 or 0.5 indicates high level of income inequality. Also, economic freedom is put at 1.15, indicating very poor economic freedom for business to thrive.

The growth rate of 6.4 percent indicates a positive sign to sustained development if growth is sustained even at that rate. It should be noted that many developed countries of the world have found it very difficult to revert to high growth rates as is experienced by Nigeria after the world economic recession of 2008.

Table 2.2 also shows that GDP per capita grew from $547 in 1950 to $1,120 in 1973 and plummeted to $852.52 in 2008. This goes on to further strengthen the prediction on how the economy failed, with the clear indication that the country's population below poverty line was 70 percent and the population under $1 a day was 70.2 percent as of 2008.

By 2008, public debt had grown to 14.4 percent of GDP, while ease of doing business index rose to a high uncomfortable level of108.

To further worsen Nigeria's economic situation, the informal sector economy was indicated to be too strong and big in the economy, with no vision of migrating to organized small scale industries and institutions, as shown in Table 2.2 as 57.9 percent of the economy.

Table 2.2 Further Nigerian Economic Data

S/N	Economic/Social Indicator	Situation as of 2008
1	Aid as percent of GDP	0.4 percent
2	Gini Index	43.7
3	Economic Freedom	1.15
4	GDP Real Growth Rate	6.4 percent
5	GDP per Capita 1950	$547.00
6	GDP per Capita 1973	$1,120.00
7	Population below Poverty line	70 percent
8	Public Debt	14.4 percent of GDP
9	Ease of Doing Business Index	108
10	GDP per Capita 2008	$852.52
11	Informal Economy	57.9 percent
12	Population under $1 a day	70.2 percent

Sources: CIA World Fact Book, 18 Dec. 2003 to Dec. 2008; Organization for Economic Cooperation and Development (2002); World Bank Development Indicators Database (2005).

Chapter 3

NIGERIA'S OIL AND GAS INDUSTRY

3.1 Background

The pride of Nigeria as a major producer of sweet crude in the world is occasioned by the huge deposit of crude oil in the Niger Delta. To date, only the Niger fields have produced all the crude oil that bring revenue to the country. The Niger Delta Region is thus seen as the threshold of Nigeria's crude oil. This section will therefore take a look at the various productive fields of the Niger Delta that makes Nigeria stand out as a major player in the international crude oil market.

3.2 Nigeria's Crude Oil Threshold: The Niger Delta

In Table 3.1, the various fields where the oil-producing companies produce crude oil in the Niger Delta are shown. Data in the Table shows that Shell BP has the highest number of field operations (mostly on-shore), including Bonga, Bomu, Nembe, Cawthorne Channel, Forcados, Imo Rivers, Jones Creek and Nembe Creek. Following Shell BP is Exxon Mobil, which operates Edop, Erha, and Ubit fields. It should be noted that Exxon Mobil is second to Shell BP in terms of size and production capacity.

Table 3.1—OIL OPERATORS AND RESERVES IN NIGERIA

S/N	OPERATOR	FIELDS	RESERVES (mmbbls)
1	Shell	Bonga	600
		Bonga South West	600
		Bomu	875
		Cawthorne Channel	750
		Forcados-Yokri	1,235
		Imo River	875
		Jones Creek	900
		Nembe Creek	950
2	Mobil	Edop	733
		Erha	1,200
		Ubit	945
3	Chevron Texaco	Agbami	1,000
		Delta	300
		Meren	1,100
		Apoi-North-Funiwa	500
		Okan	800
4	Agip	Ebegoro	160
5	TotalFinaElf	Amenam-Kpono	500
		Akpo	200
		Obagi	670

Source: Viston Communications Ltd.

It is interesting to note the reserve capacity of the various oil fields. This indicates that crude oil is a non-renewable natural resource. When the reserve is exhausted, production activity will cease in such fields, thus firms will exit investment. This had been a strong point of argument by host communities while demanding for benefits from oil companies and government in recent times. Although this situation had since been there, the awareness of communities on reserves and life span of the product in their communities had been more pronounced in recent times. Such awareness is more inspired by the post oil production status of Oloibiri community of Bayelsa State.

Table 3.1 shows that Shell Petroleum Development Company of Nigeria is the biggest player in the oil business in Nigeria. It has the largest oil reserves in the country. It has been argued, however, that due to the activities of the Niger Delta militants, Shell has shut in over half of its production capacity. Even with the current cessation of hostile activities by these militants, Shell is said to be cautious in re-opening the shut-in wells. Although Mobil is far below Shell in terms of reserves, Mobil is currently topping the producers' list of crude oil for exports among the multinational oil corporations in Nigeria. This is argued to be caused by Mobil's concentration on its offshore production activities, as its reserves are mostly located offshore. With negligible or no activities of militants in the offshore oil operations in Nigeria, Mobil has stepped up its production recently to leverage the reduction in production by Shell caused by the activities of militant restive youths in the Niger Delta Region of Nigeria. This explains part of the reasons why oil firms are now more interested in developing offshore than on-shore facilities.

The lopsidedness in the development of the Niger Delta, which is perceived by the people of the region as insincerity on the part of the central government and the central government's decision to perpetually milk the Niger Delta dry by under-developing her, bearing in mind that the area will be left desolate after oil exploration has engendered new consciousness and survival strategies in the people of the region, especially the youths, to at least exist. Many strategies have been tried out by the most vulnerable in the region—youth and women—to also capture some benefits from the bourgeoning oil sector in their lands. Such strategies have been indicated to include both legitimate and illegitimate ones.

Recent outcries by government and oil companies showed that the people have resorted more frequently to illegitimate and illegal means to derive benefits from the oil sector, which government and oil companies complain is detrimental to the growth of the economy, individual profits of the oil companies, and workplace security and safety. The commonest tool used by these youths and women, government and oil companies complain, is said to be violence, which necessarily ushers an atmosphere of restiveness. It is therefore this restiveness that has recently become a phenomenon in describing the character of the Niger Delta youths that this book intends to investigate its essence and possible mitigating variables.

Corroborating and adding to the submission of the hardcore oil industry data, reported earlier in this book, a Niger Delta activist, Dede, in his lecture at a seminar in 2009, stated that there are 6,000 oil wells in the Niger Delta, derived from 606 oil fields. He also posited that there are 1,500 Niger Delta communities hosting these fields, 275 flow stations, 10 gas plants, and 7000km of oil pipeline.

Dede further submitted that even while it has been variously noted and accepted that oil exploration in Nigeria started in Oloibiri, with all its pride of place in the "Oil's Hall of Fame" in Nigeria, Oloibiri whose status today is non-oil-producing had been left raped by NNPC and handed over to the museum's management for artifacts collection and preservation, with no remarkable development whatsoever to show its status as the community that provided the wealth Nigeria used in growing her economy and developing all the cities she has today.

3.3 Nigeria's Crude Oil Reserve and Production

Table 3.2 shows the total crude oil reserve and production in Nigeria. It could be seen that crude reserve in Nigeria rose from 24,000 millions of barrels in 2001 to 27,200 million barrels of crude oil in 2002. This reserve value, however, dropped in 2003 to 25,000 million barrels. This value drop might have been occasioned by the confirmatory national and international oil and gas reserves audit in the world that was carried out in the period.

Also from Table 3.2, oil production rate per day averaged at 2 million (2.199 million in 2001, 2.013 million in 2002, and 2.275 million in 2003). It is interesting to note that daily production of crude oil instead of growing with increased reserve as experienced recently in Nigeria kept shrinking. By 2008, the daily crude oil production in Nigeria had fallen to average 1.5 million barrels per day. This indicates a radical departure from the norm, showing that the variables that might have caused this situation or scenario are either

Table 3.2—Most of Nigeria's Oil Production and Consumption

	U.M	2001	2002	2003	percent on Total Reserve in Africa	percent on Total Reserve in the World
Reserves	millions Of barrels	24,000	27,200	25,000	29 percent	2 percent
Production	Thousand Barr p/ day	2,199	2,013	2,275	26 percent	3 percent

Source: Eni World Oil and Gas Review 2004

uncontrollable or significantly stochastic. A release by the federal government in Nigeria in 2009 had corroborated this argument of unintended reduction in daily crude production capacity by almost a million barrels of oil. This has been principally attributed to shut-ins by oil companies occasioned by violence and attacks by armed militants and communal disturbances.

Table 3.2 further shows the performance of Nigeria in the global oil economy. Due to the discovery of new oil fields, Nigeria's crude oil reserve increased from 24,000 million barrels to 27,200 million barrels in 2002. However, daily production reduced from 2.199mb/d to 2.013mb/d. In Contrast, though, reserves dropped in 2003 to 25,000 million barrels with daily production increasing to 2.275mb/d. The production regime might have been influenced by Organization of Petroleum Exporting Countries (OPEC) that takes major decisions on members" crude production quota to influence international crude oil prices (indicating supply side management strategies).

Table 3.2 also shows that Nigeria hold 29 percent of the total crude oil reserve in Africa and 2 percent of World's crude oil share. Also, by its production figure between 2001 and 2003, Nigeria produced 2 percent of world's crude and 3 percent of Africa's crude daily.

3.4 Oil Block Allocation in Nigeria

About 47 companies were listed as winners of the second bidding round concessions of the oil blocks in Nigeria. As shown in Table 3.3 below, the listed companies own the concessions in the various basins as indicated.

Table 3.3—Winners of Second Bidding Round Concession

S/N	Name of Company	Concession Held	Basin
1	Alfred James Nig. Ltd.	OPL-302	Benin
2	Amalgamated Oil	OPL-452	Niger
3	Atlas Petroleum	OPL-75	Niger
4	British Petroleum/ Statoil	OPL-213, 217, 218	Niger
5	Cavendish Petroleum	OPL-453	Niger
6	Chevron Nig	OPL-801, 805, 810, 820, 812, 818, 822	Benue
7	Chevron Nig.	OPL – 46-55, 89-95,97	Niger
8	Conoco (Du Point)	OPL-220	Niger
9	Consolidated Oil Ltd	OPL – 112, 458	Benue
10	Dubri Oil	OML – 96	Niger
11	Exxon	OPL – 209	

(Continued)

S/N	Name of Company	Concession Held	Basin
12	Allied Energy	OPL – 210	
13	Elf Nig Ltd	OPL – 447, 93, 95 – 97	Niger
14	Elf Nig Ltd	OML – 99, 102	Niger
15	Elf Nig.Ltd	OPL – 222, 223, 802, 807	Chad
16	Elf Nig Ltd	OML – 56 – 59	Chad
17	Express Pet & Gas Co.	OPL- 74	Niger
18	Mobil Producing	OPL – 94, 221	Niger
19	Mobil Producing	OML – 67-70	Niger
20	Moncrief Oil	OPL – 471	Niger
21	Nig Agip Oil Co	OPL-228,221,316	Benue
22	Nig Agip Oil Co	OPL-808,811,818	Benue
23	Nig Agip Oil Co	823, 824, 829, 830, 836	Niger
24	Nig Agip Oil Co	OLL-60-63	Benin
25	IPEC General Oil	OPL-304	Niger
26	Inko Petroleum	OPL-224	Niger
27	Nigus	OPL-496	Niger
28	NNPC/AERN	OPL-472	Niger
29	NNPC/ASHLAND	OPL-90, 98, 118, 225	Niger
30	NNPC/(DES)	N/A	Chad
31	NNPC/SUNLINK	OPL-474	Niger
32	NOREAST	OPL-215	Niger
33	NOREAST	OPL-840	Benue

(Continued)

S/N	Name of Company	Concession Held	Basin
34	NOREAST	OPL-902	Chad
35	NPDC	OPL-91,110	Niger
36	NPDC	OML-64-66	Niger
37	OPIC	OPL-208	Niger
38	PACLANTIC	OPL-204	Niger
39	PAN OCEAN	OML-98	Niger
40	Queen Petroleum	OML-135	Niger
41	Seagull	OPL-230	Niger
42	SHELL	OPL-803,806,809	Benue
43	SHELL	OPL-212,219	Niger
44	SHELL	OML-1,4,5,7,11-46	Niger
45	SHELL	71-74,76,77,79,81	Niger
46	SOLGAS NIG	OML-226	Niger
47	SUMMIT OIL	SUMMIT OIL	Niger
48	TEXACO	OPL-460	Niger
49	TEXACO	OML-83-88	Niger
50	Ultramar Energy Intl	OPL-227	Niger
51	Union SG Petrogas	OPL-201	Niger
52	Yinka Folawiyo	OPL-309	Benue

Source: Nigeria's Crude Export Terminals

It is interesting to note that from the allocations above, there are no aboriginal Niger Delta companies that are listed as holding concessions in the major oil blocks in Nigeria. This goes to show the lack of participation of the people of the region in the exploitation and exploration of oil activities that takes place in her environment. This might have been responsible for their difficulty in understanding the explanations of the oil companies on their responsibilities to the people or owners of the land that holds the resources (oil and gas) they are exploiting and their disagreement with the federal or central government on who should have the lion share of the earnings that comes

Chapter 4

THE NIGER DELTA AND ITS RESOURCES

4.1 Background

The huge economic potentials of the Niger Delta have not been exhaustively tapped. There is a polarized utilization of available resources with the scale tilting in favour of oil and gas. In this section of the paper, we highlight these abundant renewable and non-renewable resources of great economic potentials under four sub-heads, namely, minerals, agriculture, and marine and forest resources.

The area called Niger Delta is a low-lying land of innumerable creeks, waterways, and mangrove swamps that stretches for over three hundred miles from the Benin River in the west to the Cross River in the east. It covers a land area of about 26,000km² and has an estimated population of over 10 million (National Population Commission, 1991).

The Niger Delta is unique by virtue of its size (nearly 26,000km²), its location and its origin. Although it is situated in one of the wettest places on earth, it is fed by a river that passes largely through the Sahel and dry Savannah landscapes—geologically, some of the oldest on earth (Ashton Jones 1998:51).

The Niger Delta can be described in terms of relief structure, local climate, hydrology, soils, natural vegetation, natural animal communities and natural ecosystem because all these features influence the culture, occupation, social structure, resource mobilization, and utilization in what has been considered the world largest wetland located far southward in Nigeria.

By its geological setting, the landscape of the Niger Delta has undergone vast changes and continues to develop over time (Ashton Jones, 1998).

View of the Niger Delta from space. North is on the left.

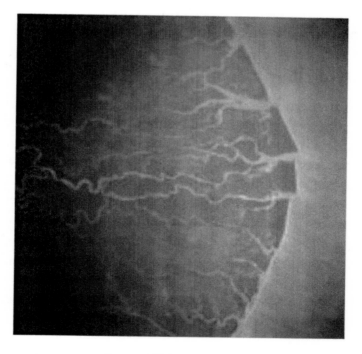

Source: Wikipedia (2008)

This text adopts and adapts the geological setting of the Niger Delta in the manner of Jones (1998).

4.2 The Climate

The Niger Delta is characterized by the tropical hot monsoon climate, especially around the Bight of Biafra, including the lower Cross River Basin and the southwesterly slopes of Mount Cameroon.

The Niger Delta lies on latitude 5 degrees north of the equator and extends into the Gulf of Guinea, dividing the Bight of Benin (to the west) from the Bight of Biafra (to the east). Annual rainfall is high although it varies within the Delta. Heavy rains begin in February and falls until November, with peaks in July through September.

4.3 Hydrology

The water structure of the Niger Delta is made of two water types, the fresh water, which is either white or black, and the brackish water, which lies in between the fresh water regime and the oceanic salt-water regime. The fresh water refers to the water coming into the Delta from the Niger/Benue river system bringing with it the sediment from the interior that makes it cloudy. This sediment dropped over time has formed the Delta itself. Another element of Niger Delta hydrology is the brackish water, which is salty as a result of the incursion of the seawater. The influence of this seawater on the Niger Delta environment extends up to 60km inland, from northeast of Sapele (on the Benin river), northeast of Warri and as far as Choba (on the New Calabar River).

4.4 The Soil

Soil is a major factor in human ecosystem that determines the viability or otherwise of the system, chiefly because man depends on the products of the soil for survival. The Niger Delta Region is endowed with very rich alluvial soil structure that supports swamp agriculture in most cases.

4.5 Mineral Resources

There is an abundant reserve of mineral resources of high economic value on land and in the waters of the Niger Delta. These constitute the non-renewable resources in the region, and include a wide variety of solid minerals, crude oil and natural gas.

4.5.1 Solid Minerals

Despite the seeming renewed enthusiasm in solid mineral development in Nigeria such abundant resources in the Niger Delta Region are still largely untapped. Exploitable solid minerals found in the region include sand, clay, salt, limestone, coal, silver, nitrate, etc. Among the lot, sand, clay and salt seem to gain more prominence, but are still largely under-utilized. However, sand is next to oil and gas on the scale of tapped minerals in the region. It is extracted massively from the extensive riverbeds, which characterize the region, and used for land reclamation, brick making, and as raw materials in the glass industry. It has great economic potentials that if well developed could support industrial activities and create employment opportunities for the teeming youths of the region. Presently, for example, only one known glass industry located at Ughelli, Delta state is on ground to utilize the abundant sand resources in the region.

Large deposits of fine kaolinite clay are also found throughout the region. This mineral with its potential in ceramic and local pottery industries is still largely untapped. A large quantity of this mineral is found in Akwa Ibom State and the Ceramics Industry of Akwa Ibom State was established due to the availability of this resource in commercial quantity there.

The abundance of marine water resource in the Niger Delta presents an untapped potential in salt production. However, such ventures are yet to be established for large-scale economic benefits.

4.5.2 Crude Oil

Crude oil is the most extensively exploited mineral resource in Nigeria. Crude oil was discovered in commercial quantity in Nigeria, in Oloibiri, a community in Bayelsa state, in 1956. Since then, enormous deposits of the mineral have been found on-shore and offshore in every part of the Niger Delta Region where all of the nation's oil is tapped. By 1997 Nigeria's proven oil reserve was put at 15.5 billion barrels. There are three known giant oil reserves with potential for 1 billion barrels production located in the region, namely the Nembe creek, Gbarain (Bayelsa) and Okan (Akwa Ibom) fields. Exploration and production activities are unceasing, with over 2 million barrels of crude oil produced daily from the Niger Delta. Nigeria thus contributes about 10 percent of the world's light crude oil, which is highly valued for high yield of light oil products and low sulfur content.

Crude oil has thus been the object of a monolithic economy, with revenues accounting for 25 percent of GDP, 90 percent of foreign exchange earnings and 70 percent of budgetary expenditure (Ministry of Finance, 2004).

4.5.3 Natural Gas

Natural gas is second to crude oil on the list of exploited mineral resources in the Nigeria's Niger Delta Region. Nigeria's natural gas reserve is put at about 124 Trillion Standard Cubic Feet (SCF). Enormous proportion of this remains and is produced in association with oil. About 4.07 Billion SCF of such associated gas is produced in the Niger Delta oil fields daily as by-product of oil exploration; and about 70.23 percent of this is currently flared. However, while great environmental and economic concerns linger against continued gas flaring, hope for commercial exploitation of gas remains in the three major gas projects, namely, SPDC Associated Gas Gathering Project, Chevron Escravos Gas Project (EGP), Exxon-Mobil Osso Natural Gas Liquid project (Osso NGL), and the Nigeria Liquefied Natural Gas project (NNLG). With these projects, currently flared gas would be processed for local use in various industrial and domestic power generation applications, as well as for export.

The abundant reserve of natural gas in the Niger Delta thus presents viable investment opportunities in the gas industry, e.g., in gas plants development for production of domestic cooking and industrial gases; and would create jobs for the unemployed. Presently about 1.17 percent of the gas reserve has been produced.

4.6 Agricultural Resources

Agriculture represents a major aspect of the renewable natural resources sector of the Nigeria economy. The Niger Delta Region is blessed with abundant soil resource with extensive arable farmland, which supports subsistence agriculture and presents enormous potentials for agro-based industrial development. In every part of the region, the arable farmland supports production of a variety of food and cash crops including cassava, yam, cocoyam, rice, maize, plantain, oil palm, raffia palm, coconut, cocoa, mango, rubber, etc. There are major food and cash crops, which are in high abundance, and could be processed into high-demand products for local and export needs, or serve as raw materials for a variety of agro-based industries. Some of such crops are highlighted here:

4.6.1 Cassava (*Manihot esculenta*)

Cassava is widely grown in the region mostly for production of garri, fufu, starch, and tapioca. It is a ready raw material for industrial starch, which could serve the needs of textile, drug and paper industries. Extensive cassava farming, processing and industrial applications for local need and export thus represent a viable investment potential that needs to be harnessed.

4.6.2 Rice (*Oryza sativa*)

Rice is a staple food and most rapidly growing food source in Africa. Land and water resources are abundantly available and adequate for rice production in the region. The wetlands and swamps are conducive for the cultivation of wet (or swamp) rice.

4.6.3 Oil Palm (*Elaeis guineensis*)

Oil palm trees are the most ubiquitous tree crop in the Niger Delta Region. Wild palm groves are the major source of edible oil. The abundance of this cash crop provides a potential for large-scale investment in palm oil processing and allied industries for both local and export needs. Oil and kernel derived from oil palm are high-demand raw materials for various industrial applications, Iing foods, cosmetics/detergents, industrials oils, etc.

4.6.4 Raffia Palm (*Raphia sp*)

Raffia palms, from which palm wine is tapped, grow extensively in the swamps of the Niger Delta. They are also grown in the homestead in most communities. Its abundance presents a great potential for industrial development in the areas of palm wine bottling, distillery for production of export quality gin, industrial alcohol production, and dry yeast production for baking and medical applications. The tree also produces piassava, another major commodity of the 1850s Atlantic trade, which still has export value today and could also support the twine industry among others.

4.6.5 Rubber Tree (*Hevea brasilensis*)

Rubber is a common tree crop in most part of the Niger Delta. It grows as a forest resource, and also grown in plantations. There is great industrial demand for latex from rubber for production of plastics and glue for the wood and paper industries. Rubber latex is also useful in tyre manufacturing. The development of rubber cultivation/production would thus provide raw materials for local rubber processing factories and for the export market.

4.7 Forest Resources

The Niger Delta is located in the tropical rainforest zone. It has the largest area of undisturbed forest in Nigeria. The region is blessed with vast array of fresh water swamp as well as mangrove forests on the upland and coastal zones. These forests constitute the natural ecosystem for diverse plant and animal species, hiding very rare flora and fauna.

The major economic potentials of the forest resources lie on timber and non-timber forest products. A variety of commercially important timber species are found in abundance in the region, e.g., Iroko (*Milicia excelsa*), Cotton tree (*Ceiba pentandra*), Mahogany (*Khaya sp*) and Mangrove (*Rhizophora sp*).

The forests also provide a variety of commonly hunted animal species, e.g., grass cutters, antelopes, bears, and hares; also, medicinal roots, leaves, barks, fruits and spices, canes and ropes, honey, etc. However, timber is the most exploited forest resource in the region, although great opportunities still abound for development of investments in this area.

4.8 Marine Resources

The aquatic terrain of the Niger Delta is unique, and characterizes the region as a resource base of the nation. This provides great potential in fisheries. A wide variety of fish and shell with other seafood of high value and importance are abundant (e.g., mackerels, threadfins, croakers, periwinkle, oysters, and scallops), enabling opportunities for fresh and coastal marine zones fishing.

The estuaries in the Niger Delta have deep-sea channels that have potentials for the development of the seaports. Currently, the Calabar Port/Export Processing Zone (EPZ) and other ports at Onne, Koko, Bonny, and Sapele are rendering tremendous stimulus to the Nigerian economy.

Akwa Ibom State, however, currently claims the endowment of the deepest natural seashore at Ibaka in Mbo local government area, which the state government is bidding to develop into an international seaport status.

4.9 Natural Resource Endowment (by States)

Table 4.1 concisely shows the natural resource endowments of the Niger Delta Region by states. It shows how rich the Niger Delta Region is and how nature have generously distributed its resources among its constituent states. It could be easily inferred that apart from oil, natural gas, condensate, and its related resources, there are also other numerous resources of bountiful economic value in the region. For instance, Uranium, which is a key constituent in nuclear energy development process, is commercially available in Akwa Ibom, Bayelsa, and Cross River. This is aside other very notable minerals found as recorded in the states of the region.

Table 4.1—Natural Resource Endowment (by States)

S/N	STATES	RESOURCE ENDOWMENT
1	Akwa Ibom	Clay, Lead/Zinc, Lignite, Limestone, Oil/Gas, Salt, Uranium
2	Bayelsa	Clay, Gypsum, Lead/Zinc, Lignite, Limestone, Manganese, Oil/Gas, Uranium
3	Cross River	Baryte, Lead/Zinc, Lignite, Manganese, Oil/Gas, Salt, Uranium
4	Delta	Clay, Glass-Sand, Gypsum, Iron-ore, Kaolin, Lignite, Marble

(Continued)

Table 4.1—*(Continued)*

S/N	STATES	RESOURCE ENDOWMENT
5	Edo	Bitumen, Clay, Dolomite, Phosphate, Glass-Sand, Gold, Gypsum, Iron-ore, Lignite, Limestone, Marble, Oil/Gas
6	Rivers	Clay, Glass-Sand, Lignite, Marble, Oil/Gas
7	Abia	Gold, Lead/Zinc, Limestone, Oil/Gas, Salt
8	Imo	Gypsum, Lead/Zinc, Lignite, Limestone, Marcasite, Oil/Gas, Phosphate, Salt
9	Ondo	Bitumen, Clay, Coal Dimension Stone, Feldspar, Gemstone, Glass-Sand, Granite, Gypsum, Kaolin, Limestone, Bauxite, Oil/Gas

Source: Akpan, O. (2011)

Chapter 5

THE SOCIO-ECONOMICS OF THE NIGER DELTA

5.1 Background

The Niger Delta Region is that part of Nigeria defined by the delta of the Niger River in Nigeria. The recent population census in Nigeria shows that the Niger Delta Region is a densely populated area with a total figure of about 31 million or 20.6 percent of the Nigerian population, for the 9 politically defined Niger Delta states (including Abia, Akwa Ibom, Bayelsa, Cross River, Delta, Edo, Imo, Ondo and Rivers). This region before now was called the Oil Rivers because it was once a major producer of palm oil. The area was the British Oil Rivers Protectorate from 1885 until 1893, when it was expanded and it became the Niger Coast Protectorate.

The South-South Niger Delta includes Akwa Ibom State, Bayelsa State, Cross River State, Delta State, Edo State, and Rivers State. During the colonial period, the core Niger Delta was a part of Eastern Region of Nigeria that came into being in 1951 (one of the three regions, and later one of the four Regions). This region included the people from colonial Calabar and Ogoja Divisions, which are the present Ogoja, Annang, Ibibio, and the Efik people, the

Igbo people, and the Ijaw, with Igbo as the majority and the NCNC (National Council of Nigeria and Cameroon) as the ruling political party in the region. NCNC later became the National Convention of Nigerian Citizens after Western Cameroon decided to cut-away from Nigeria and became a part of Cameroon.

Although there were several movements for the creation and recognition of ethnic minorities in the Nigerian Federation, even prior to independence, these struggles started crystallising for the creation of the Niger Delta Region in 1953 in the old Eastern region when a major crisis that led to the expulsion of Professor Eyo Ita from office by the majority tribe of the old eastern region took place. The minorities in the region, mainly people of the old Calabar Kingdom, the Ijaw and Ogoja demanded a state or region of their own, specifically, the Calabar-Ogoja-Rivers (COR) State. The struggle for the creation of COR state continued and was a major issue on the status of minorities in Nigeria during debates in Europe for Nigerian independence.

Further agitation and struggle for the recognition of the South Eastern Nigeria minorities saw the declaration of an Independent Niger Delta Republic by Isaac Adaka Boro during Ironsi's administration, just before the civil war.

During the Nigerian civil war (1966–1970), the Nigerian government saw the need to accept the request of the South Eastern Region minorities to create them out of South Eastern region. However, instead of the regional structure of governance practiced in the country before the war, the government decided to have a state structure while jettisoning the regional structure. Therefore, instead of the COR State demanded by the minorities of the South East, the federal government created South Eastern and Rivers states. South Eastern State had the colonial Calabar Division (old Calabar Kingdom), and colonial Ogoja Division. South Eastern State and River State became two states for the minorities of the old eastern region, and the majority Igbo of the old eastern region had a state called East Central State. South Eastern State was renamed Cross River State and was later split into Cross River State and Akwa Ibom State. Rivers State was later divided into Rivers State and Bayelsa State.

The next phase of the Niger Delta struggle saw the request for justice and the end of marginalization of the Niger Delta people, and the cessation of the environmental rape of the area by the Nigerian government with Ken Saro Wiwa as the lead figure for this phase of the struggle. The acute lack of development in the region and the robust sensitization of the people on what rights they had to ask for their rights and even seek redress resulted in coordinated agitation for equity and participation by the Niger Delta people in the oil produced in their communities and grounds. They also complained about environmental pollution and destruction of their land and rivers by oil companies. Ken Saro Wiwa and other leaders were later consumed in the struggle.

Unfortunately, though, we are today witnessing a Niger Delta struggle that has gone out of control, becoming more militant in nature with some taints of criminality imported into a genuine struggle.

The core Niger Delta states is therefore defined as the Southernmost states of the Nigerian Federation, including Akwa Ibom, Bayelsa, Cross River, Delta, Edo and Rivers (South-South Economic Summit, 2009). This monolithic Niger Delta explained by the six southernmost State structure is here further subdivided into two major zones thus:

55

5.1.1 Western Niger Delta

The Western Niger Delta consists of the western section of the coastal South-South Nigeria that includes Delta and Edo states. The western Niger Delta is a heterogeneous society with several ethnic groups with Ijaw as the majority. Other ethnic groups include Urhobo, Ezon, Isoko, Itsekiri, and Ukwuani (Igbo). Their livelihoods are primarily based on fishing and farming. History has it that the Western Niger was controlled by chiefs of five separate powerful nations with whom the British government had to sign separate "Treaties of Protection" with in their formation of "Protectorates" that later became southern Nigeria. The five Chiefs were the Chiefs of Itsekiri, Isoko, Ukwuani, Ijaw, and Urhobo.

5.1.2 Eastern Niger Delta

The Eastern Niger Delta consists of the eastern section of the coastal South Nigeria that includes: Bayelsa, Rivers, Akwa Ibom, and Cross River states. The Eastern Niger Delta Region has the Ibibios, Ijaws, Efiks, Annang, Oron, and the Ekoi (Ogoja) people, of old Calabar Kingdom, who are all related with a common language and ancestors, the Ogoni and some Igbo groups (that consists of the Ekpeye, Ndoni, Etche, Ikwerre, Ndoki, Ogba-Egbema subgroups) in Rivers State and in Delta State.

5.2 Occupation of the Niger Delta

We have already surveyed the Niger Delta environment and examined its natural and human ecosystem. Having been familiar with the ecosystem, and its resources, which include fertile soil, fish, timber, oil and gas, oil palm and rubber, raffia and craft, periwinkle, etc., it will leave us with no difficulty to explain the economic life of these people.

Conditioned by the characteristic rainforest, porous sandy soil, and a network of rivers and creeks, the Niger Delta people are traditionally hunters, farmers, fishermen, palm oil, wine and gin producers, and canoe makers.

However, since the discovery of oil in commercial quantities more than four decades ago, there have been somewhat less intensification of the people in their traditional occupation. The massive exploration and exploitation of oil with its negative impact on the environment has led to the collapse of the traditional economy thus putting these fishermen and farmers out of job. In its place, a generation of restive, unemployed able-bodied youths now put the region under anxiety and in some cases angst.

But amidst this emerging scenario, a typical Niger Deltan is still a farmer and fisherman, eking out a living from the waters, which have become less productive with increasing degradation of the ecosystem.

However, in communities where fishing is still the major occupation, it is done mostly inshore. Inshore fishing could extend from inland waters to 70km from the coast. The fishermen use powered boats propelled by outboard motors while others paddle their canoes into the rivers, creeks and the sea to fish with fishing nets that are sometimes stretched between two fishing boats. Some fishermen use lines and hooks while some, especially, those after shellfish such as lobsters, crabs and crayfish use wicker baskets, which they lower into the water and leave for sometimes.

5.3 Social Structure

We have already identified the principal people of the Niger Delta as the Urhobo, Itsekiri, Ijaw, Ibibio, Efik, and some traces of Igbo stock. Nevertheless, other smaller and numerous ethnic groups are subsumed in these principal groups.

The social structure of Niger Delta is a product of history, tradition and socio-political experience and the Niger Delta city-states as they were earlier structured had the models of kingdoms, house systems and village. Such social structure was greatly shaped by their experience of slave trade and social disruptions of revolutions, over the centuries. Notwithstanding all explained constituent parts (ethnic groups) of the Niger Delta, the region was dominated by five city-states as described in Webster and Boahey (1967).

Each city-state was made up of three parts: the capital, its hearts and nerve centre, its colonies of satellite villages and its trading empire, in the oil belt of the interior. Since the capital cities were located in the mangrove swamps, agriculture or transportation, with the growth in European demand for slaves in the seventeenth and eighteenth centuries, the capital cities had reached out, ignoring the land but striving to control the harbours and creeks, the fishing grounds and the water ways to the interior.

5.4 Settlement Pattern

The Niger Delta is predominantly a rural settlement usually called a village. Bannet and Okurotifa (1984) identifies three types of village settlement namely: dispersed settlement that may be a single house; nucleated settlement in which a group of houses are clustered together and linear or elongated settlement that may consist of a line of houses along a road, a river, the edge of a line of houses along a road, a river, the edge of a swamp or the edge of a forest. Because of the nature of its environment village settlement in the Niger Delta falls under the elongated type, especially where fishing activities occur along the banks of the distributaries in the Niger Delta.

5.5 The Culture

Culture is an aggregate of the people's history, tradition, values, practices, and belief systems. Like any other society the states of the Niger Delta have a system of traditional practices, values, behavioral and belief systems that have been identified with them over the years.

Unlike the western states that had a common history, tradition and customs the culture of the Niger Delta have same variations, though they produce similar indicators because of the similarities in their socio-political and economic experience and by circumstance of geography. We have already identified the main people of the Niger Delta. But what constitutes their cultural values?

The Ijaw, Ibibio, and Efik have had some cultural similarities and similar institutions. Key elements in the Kingdom of Warri, in the Western Delta, for instance, do not really resemble the Ijaw, Ibibio, and Efik. Rather, the Itsekiri of Warri have much more in common with the Edo of Benin and their Yoruba neighbours.

Unlike in the forest zone where empires and kingdoms developed, large states were not an emergent feature of the Delta. Instead, the Ijaw and Efik were organized into age groups by village, forming the major institutions of government.

The presence of and use of Ekpe society has brought additional dimensions to the cultural and political institutions in Efik. In old Calabar (Efik), Ekpe secret society was an important political tool. Wealthy men of old families exercised authority by buying their way into Ekpe. Ekpe society grew more powerful because an ambitious freeman of means could not achieve real importance unless he became a member. The members of Ekpe Society, who were drawn from the various villages into which Calabar was divided, governed by virtue of their high office in society.

All these arose as a result of states struggle to monopolize the slave trade so as to obtain all the trading dues paid by European ships. Leaders needed some kind of force to emerge and therefore kept armed followers who helped to open strategic waterways, which led to the slave producing hinterland.

Ekpe society was also widely used by Ibibio especially around the Uruan area. However, the most dominant cultural and political instrument among the Ibibio was the Ekpo secret society.

The Ijaw of Bonny, Nembe, and Kalabari made use of divinities such that their kings were believed to be partly divine. The king carried deities such as Simingi, the most powerful of Bonny's four deities.

In Nembe and Kalabari, the most important secret society was called Ekine (there was no Ekine society), and it produced masquerades and plays. Ekine was socially and politically significant, because membership in the society cut across house divisors, helping to integrate houses into one political entity.

Ibibio who migrated and settled at Ikono in Uyo before they dispersed had a powerful deity called Ibritam. The

Ibritam oracle was extremely popular, and the major seven Ibibio deities can be found in the areas around Ikono in Uyo—specifically, Ikot Oku Ikono, which houses the headquarters of the Ibibio Ancestral home, the Asan Ibibio.

5.6 Other Social Infrastructure and Issues

Available figures show that there is one doctor per 82,000 people, rising to one doctor per 132,000 in some areas of the Niger Delta, especially the rural areas that is more than three times the National average of 40,000 people per Doctor. Only 27 percent of people in the Niger Delta have access to safe drinking water and about 30 percent of households have access to electricity, both of which are below the National averages of 31.7 percent and 33.6 percent respectively. Only 6 percent of the population of the Niger Delta have access to telephones, while 70 percent have never used a telephone (Ibeanu, 2006).

Apart from a federal Trunk Broad that crosses Bayelsa State, the State had only 15km of tarred road as of 2008. According to a World Bank Study in the urban areas of Rivers State, the cost of living index of 783 is the highest in Nigeria. Gross National Product (GNP) per capita is below the national average of $280, and unemployment in Port Harcourt is as high as 30 percent.

Access to education, which is indicated as being very central to remedying some of these social conditions, lags abysmally when compared to other parts of the country. While 76 percent of Nigerian children attend primary school, in the Niger Delta, the figure drops to between 30 percent and 40 percent (Ibeanu, 2006).

Chapter 6

THE ROOT CAUSES OF YOUTH RESTIVENESS IN THE NIGER DELTA REGION

6.1 Background

This chapter will discuss the root causes of restiveness in the Niger Delta. Many studies and authors have, however, chronicled some of the causes of this restiveness in the past, but interestingly, decisions based on currently identified causes of youth restiveness in the Niger Delta Region have failed to comprehensively nip in the bud the monster "restiveness" that has currently defied many solutions techniques based on current understanding of the causes of the monster in the Niger Delta Region. This text is interested in a more in-depth analysis of the situation in order to add value to the plethora of arguments concerning the root causes of youth restiveness in the Niger Delta.

This fundamental gap noticed in making policies that will contain youth restiveness in the Niger Delta further encouraged the authors of this text. With the help of researches, studies, and consultancies offered by the authors to several intervention agencies and government in the region, it was discovered that only participatory methodology of data gathering could unlock the "suspicious" mindset of the stakeholders in the region, who are best located to tell the story of restiveness in the region and to suggest practical mitigating variables and enablers to youth restiveness in the region.

The lead author of this book, having worked as a development expert in the Niger Delta and in several assignment and studies within the Niger Delta Region, authoritatively identifies the burning issues constituting the root causes of youth restiveness in the Niger Delta Region, among others that were identified from other development facilitators working with participatory identification techniques also in the region.

6.2 Theoretical Issues

Restiveness in the Niger Delta can be located around issues like riots, violence, kidnappings, illegal bunkering, and arm struggles, among others. Riots had been located around seizures of oil installations and oil facilities. Notably, riots have been associated with all other indicators of youth restiveness. Events like kidnapping, seizure of oil facilities, illegal bunkering, and armed maneuvers are always either preceded or followed by riots and violence. This had made the region to be noted and branded as one of the most violent areas of the world (VOA, 2008). The Voice of America (VOA) Radio service reported in 2010 that after the Gulf of Aden, where Somalia pirates reign supreme, the second most dangerous area in international maritime navigation is the Gulf of Guinea, where the Niger Delta youth militants do not only kidnap for ransom, but kidnap to collect ransom and kill thereafter, with abounding violent and riotous tendencies.

The economic theory of riots predicts that only the private costs and benefits should determine whether the individuals participate. If the benefits of the group of rioters are important, it is because of a link between them and private benefits to each rioter (Carreyou, 2005).

If we argue in the manner of Edwards (2007), taking the position that the opportunity costs of time and the likely costs of punishment influence the eruption and intensity of the riots, we can here say that the Niger Delta restiveness marked by violence and riots among others is not totally captured by this theoretical frame. The restive youths of the Niger Delta from their operational mode, rather than consider costs of punishment, consider taking higher risk for higher returns. Their actions is indicative of the consideration that the higher the risk they take, ignoring whatever might be the consequence of reaction from the law enforcement, they will get higher returns. For instance, the kidnap of high profile oil workers from their depots, which are heavily protected by the armed forces, as well as invading and violently taking over oil installations like flow stations and oil pipelines, may fetch more financial returns notwithstanding the costs or punishment that their action may attract.

Edwards (2007) argues further that large, urban centers host more riots than smaller ones, because it is easier to organize unrest in large cities than in small, rural towns. That cities offer the following advantages to rioters: reduction in the mobility of law enforcement because of congestion, rapid access to information, and ease of strategic coordination. In the Niger Delta case, a differential scenario offers itself. Even when the Niger Delta is a rural setting, riotous and violent situations outside the city centers thrive because of the difficult terrain and access to the rural communities that host the all-important oil installations by law enforcement. The rapid growth of telecommunication facilities in the country and in the Niger Delta had also offered itself rapid access to information and strategic coordination.

DiPasquale and Glaeser (1998) assumed that a population receives a range of net benefits from rioting, which include all the benefits and costs of rioting except those specifically linked to financing police. That the desire to participate in a riot does not only come primarily from individual benefits (stolen goods and merchandise), but also from the political benefits that will be reaped by the group and internalized by individuals within the group. The case of individual benefit as precursor to involve in riot could be seen in the restive groups in the Niger Delta who often than not break into splinter units once benefits captured have not been justifiably (in the individual's thinking) shared among members of the group. Cases of intra squabbles and violence after loots by these restive groups have been variously reported in the Niger Delta.

In the case of some restive groups of the Niger Delta that were considered in governmental and other formal quarters (including the international community) as criminals, they are very well organized, some ideologically based while others are bound together by pecuniary interest. Edwards (2007) see organized crime groups as quasi-governments, similar in structure and economic impact to predatory states and emerging from a power vacuum created by the absence of state enforcement. In many cases, the lack of police protection could be geographic, social, or ethnic, or due to prohibition. In the Niger Delta, groups like this exist. The ones that are most feasible and organized like MEND and NPDV among others are currently in discussions with the Nigerian government on amnesty issues after the federal government of Nigeria decided to adopt non-military format in negotiating with armed militants in the Niger Delta Region. The disadvantage, though, in the crime market as brought out by Edwards (2007) is that organized crime creates monopolies for criminal activity out of a perfectly competitive market. For instance, in the Niger Delta, when kidnapping was very competitive among market actors in the Niger Delta, any small group of criminals could come together to plan and kidnap to earn ransom, but when organized groups like MEND and NPDV came into the picture with controls and somewhat ideological bent, they cornered the kidnapping market, as the small and individual groups had to report to them and commit loyalty before entering the "lucrative" kidnap market.

6.3 The Root Causes of Youth Restiveness in the Niger Delta Region

6.3.1 Location of Region

The Niger Delta Region of Nigeria is located in a very difficult geographical terrain. Communities in most cases are located in creeks and dykes. It takes the inhabitants of this environment some efforts to access their homes. Due to its difficult and inaccessible terrain, government and other development partners were not encouraged to take development there. For instance, to build a house in Ekeremor or Nembe in Bayelsa State, one needs about three times the amount one would have used in building a similar structure in Port Harcourt, Rivers State. Its inaccessibility and remoteness prompt the region to be turned into a breeding ground for criminals, who see the environment as a peaceful abode where they can disappear to after committing crimes in the cities. More encouraging to these boxed-in youths was the discovery and sitting of oil industry installations in this difficult-terrain environment.

The youth of these Niger Delta communities were overlooked by the early policies of oil prospectors (including the government as represented by Nigeria National Petroleum Corporation (NNPC) and the multinational oil companies). Also, because the government and the oil companies further ignored communities' infrastructural provisions when they were installing their infrastructures, criminal elements capitalized on the genuine agitation of communities and progressive youths to cause confusion for their criminal gains.

6.3.2 Resource Distribution

This section of the book is adapted from a study undertaken by the lead author in the Niger Delta Region. The study was particularly carried out in Mbiabet Ikpe community in Ini Local government Area of Akwa Ibom State, Egbemo Angalabiri community of Ekeremor Local government Area of Bayelsa State, Igbuku community of Ndokwa East Local government Area of Delta State, and Akasa community in Brass Local government Area of Bayelsa State. The result presented here is a derived one from several distinct studies, part of which is reported in Ekong (2007) and Ekong & Onye (2012).

These studies where the lead author participated in and draws inspiration from were sponsored severally and in particular and distinct bits by the Niger Delta Environmental Survey (NDES), Shell Petroleum Development Company of Nigeria (SPDC), Niger Delta Wetland Centre, and Northern Akwa Ibom Swamp Resources Development Study. In all of these studies, the lead author as a development facilitator lived in the communities and, using participatory methodologies, facilitated the collection of data to assess the variables on *resource distribution*, which came up strongly in the early interactions with the various communities, distinctively, on why youth restiveness persisted in their areas. It was as a result of these distinct and various studies and their findings that the lead author facilitated in some of these communities the establishment of a community savings and credit scheme as reported in Ekong (2008)—particularly in Mbiabet and Egbemo Angalabiri communities. The gap identified in funding the poor and vulnerable women and youths mostly found in the informal sector of the communities led to the establishment of the community savings and credit schemes (CS&CS) that was aimed at mobilizing local and outside funds for the vulnerable women and youths in the communities who could not access benefits from the sophisticated oil multinationals and government agencies operating in their areas, for investment in their local and traditional trades and opportunities.

The authors in those studies identified *resource distribution* as a single very effective factor that had really helped in triggering off the restiveness of youths in the Niger Delta. The authors discovered in these studies that there were two main or principal resource or benefit holders in the Niger Delta. They include the government and the multinational oil companies. While the government controls all the wealth created in the environment, the oil companies creates wealth from the oil sector for the government, while making its profit from the process. These two entities constitute the largest creators of any perceived revenue and wealth for any economic benefit in the region.

Although there are other small holding pockets of resource holders across the Niger Delta, this book, in the manner of the authors researches in the Niger Delta opines that they were too insignificant to be of any critical benefits to the yearnings and aspirations of the Niger Delta people, mostly because their source of existence depended in very many cases almost totally on government and the multinational oil companies. These include as discovered in the research the banks, small-scale businesses, and the bourgeoning informal sector.

6.3.3 Resource Beneficiaries in the Niger Delta

The study identified six main resource beneficiary groupings:

i. Business: these included banks, contractors, small-scale business operators—many in the oil-servicing sector (contractors, banks, etc.).
ii. Public/Formal Sector Employees: these included company and government workers, casual workers, company armed security, etc.
iii. Informal Sector Employees: these included, prostitutes, artisans, subsistence and small farmers, market women, small provision stores,

dealers, motorcyclists, drivers, Off/On licenses, and "419," among others.

iv. Underemployed and unemployed community class: these included youths, women, and men who are either just unemployed or underemployed. In some communities, people are paid by companies to stay at home and away from worksites for fear of causing restiveness.

v. Politicians: this constitutes the political class that governs and determines governance.

vi. Traditional Institutions: another very important sector that is responsible for governance at the grassroots level. They remain very important in many parts of the Niger Delta as they are seen as the custodians of traditional deities, customs, relics, and pride of the people.

6.3.4 The Resource Distribution Model in Niger Delta

Focus group discussions, questionnaires, and participatory observation methodologies addressing specific issues and questions seeking answer to how resources are distributed in the communities were adopted and administered on structurally arranged populations in the Niger Delta communities that the authors facilitated the reported studies. Respondents included business people, teachers, oil company workers, development workers, youths, women, community chiefs and leaders, government functionaries, and politicians from the communities. The presentation made here is a summary of all similar works done by the authors in the communities earlier mentioned.

Table 6.3.1   Resource Distribution Chain

S/N		Resource Holders/Benefit Distribution		
		Government	Multinationals	
	Beneficiaries	% Accrued Direct Benefit	% Accrued Direct Benefit	Average Total
1	Business	55	90	72.5
2	Pub/Formal Sector Emp.	15	0	7.0
3	Informal Sec. Emp.	0	0	0
4	Und/Unem. Comm. Class	2	1	1.5
5	Politicians	25	3	14.0
6	Traditional Institutions	3	6	4.5

Source: Fieldwork Survey

Table 6.3.1 indicates how resources are distributed among the identified sectors in the Niger Delta community. We can see that from the total direct benefit accruing from the government, the business sector benefits the most, getting 55 percent of such benefit. Politicians get 25 percent of the benefits, while the public/formal sector gets 15 percent of the benefits from government. While traditional rulers get 3 percent of the benefits from government, the underemployed and unemployed, maybe from transferred income or from informal association with politicians and businesses, get 2 percent of the benefit accruing from government. It is, however, interesting to note that the informal sector derives no direct benefit from government in the region.

On benefits accruing from the oil sector, the business sector gets 90 percent of the benefits from the multinational oil companies. Traditional institutions get 6 percent, as these traditional rulers are used by the oil companies to buy peace in the communities where they are producing. Politicians get only 3 percent of the benefits. This is explained by the fact that politicians in the region have no power or authority to influence the activities of the oil companies in the region, except those politicians at the centre who are handsomely rewarded with bunkering contracts and others juicy oil related contracts and contacts to keep them away from disturbing the multinationals operating in the region.

The underemployed and unemployed get 1 percent of direct benefit from the multinational oil companies, mostly through casual works, standby payments, or when oil companies are forced to undertake ransom payment for activities that is non-productive to the oil companies.

On the average, the table shows that the business sector benefits most from the accrued direct benefit of government and the oil companies at 72.5 percent, followed by politicians at 14 percent and the public/formal sector at 7 percent. Traditional institutions average 4.5 percent. The underemployed/unemployed community averages 1.5 percent, while the informal sector has 0 percent.

It could be easily deduced from the above that the sectors most visible around the operations of the oil companies and government in the region are the ones that are least benefited by the resource distribution in the resource benefit chain.

6.3.5 Resource Utilization by Beneficiaries

It is expected that all beneficiaries of government and multinationals will plough back some part of such benefits into the economy that they derived benefits from. We therefore intend here to investigate the application of these benefits from the government by beneficiaries. Table 6.3.2 shows how the earlier identified economic beneficiaries and actors in the Niger Delta Region utilized the benefits they derived from the region.

Table 6.3.2 Beneficiaries' Domiciliation of Government and Multinationals Derived Benefit

S/N	Beneficiaries	Beneficiaries Domiciliation of Benefits					
		Government		Multinationals			
		% Accrued Domiciliation		% Accrued Domiciliation		Average Total	
		ND	OND	ND	OND	ND	OND
1	Business	5	95	1	99	3	97
2	Pub/Formal Sector Emp.	75	25	-	-	75	25
3	Informal Sec. Emp.	-	-	-	-	-	-
4	Und/Unem. Comm. Class	100	-	100	-	100	
5	Politicians	3	97	1	99	2	98
6	Traditional Institutions	5	95	1	99	3	97
7	Oil Company Workers	-	-	15	85	15	85

ND – Niger Delta
OND – Outside Niger Delta
Source: Fieldwork Survey

6.3.5.1 *Government Beneficiaries' Domiciliation of Benefit*

1. Business: In the case of businesses operating in the Niger Delta, 97 percent of the profit they made was repatriated outside the region as many of them were not from the Niger Delta Region and would also not want to leave anything in the region for safety against supposed militant youths. The remaining 3 percent was spent on recurrent and other sundry issues, mostly on the purchase of peace for its operations.

2. Public/Formal Sector Employees: The formal and public sector employees operating in the region receive benefits that are too small to engender any meaningful savings and subsequent investment; thus, nearly all income made is consumed. Those in the public/formal sector that make unearned income keep it away from the view of the people by investing or keeping such earnings outside the Niger Delta Region for fear of being asked to explain the legality of the source of such earnings.

3. Informal Sector Employees: The informal sector employees seem to have no direct benefit from both benefit holders. Since they do not have direct business link with the government or multinational oil companies, they do not make any income from these sources. It is, however, important to note that many of the youths and women of the Niger Delta operate in this sector. Under/Unemployed Community

Class: Since such benefits are very meager, they are immediately consumed. Benefits here more often than not come in terms of transfer payments, rents, and compensations.

4. Politicians: politicians, because of their governmental influence, benefit from both the government and the oil companies. However, according to the study, 97 percent of the benefits they make from the government are taken out of the Niger Delta for safety purposes and for fear of being noticed.

5. Traditional Institutions: Whatever extra benefit acquired by the traditional rulers outside their stipulated stipends in the region is repatriated for safety and to keep away from the community view (in this case 95 percent), as they would be regarded "rappers" of the community for staying wealthy and close to government when their subjects are suffering.

6.3.5.2 *Multinationals Beneficiaries' Domiciliation of Benefit*

1. Business: Over 99 percent are foreign business firms (foreign here meaning businesses that are not owned by indigenes of the Niger Delta). These businesses locate their headquarters and operational offices outside the Niger Delta while only keeping liaison services points in the Niger Delta. In most cases they even default on tax to the local authorities while contributing little or nothing to the economies of their host

communities. As in Table 6.3.2 above, 99 percent of the benefits made by the business sector are repatriated out of the Niger Delta, as the business sector does not have any stake in the region.

2. Public/Formal Sector Employees: In many cases during the study reported here, a very little percentage of these had access to economic benefits of the multinational oil companies. As such, the benefit accruing was infinitesimal and not any significant.

3. Informal Sector Employees: Informal sector employees had no access at all to the economic activities of the multinational oil companies. Therefore, they derived no benefit; thus, there was no transfer of benefits.

4. Under/Unemployed Community Class: From the little they derived from the oil companies, mostly through their ingenuity, all was invested back in the region.

5. Politicians: 99 percent of benefits derived from multinational oil companies were kept outside the Niger Delta in order not to agitate the sensibilities of the locals, who see politicians as conspiring with the companies to undermine their economic rights. On average, 98 percent of the benefits they got were taken outside the Niger Delta Region.

6. Traditional Institutions: whatever benefits are acquired are repatriated for safety and to keep them away from the community view. From Table 6.2, 97 percent of their earnings were repatriated outside the Niger Delta.

7. Company Workers: those with large incomes do not reside in the Niger Delta thus they do not pay tax or contribute to the economy of the area. Only an army of small-income and casual staff of multinationals stay in the Niger Delta. Also, income made by the armed forces guarding oil installations are repatriated out. For instance, expenditures on the armed forces (equipment, logistics, and sundry items) are not domiciled in the communities.

6.3.6 Consequences of the Resource Distribution Model

6.3.6.1 Consequences of Current Benefits Distribution and Domiciliation in the Niger Delta Region

According to Table 6.3.2, overall, an average of 79 percent of benefits from both government and multinational oil companies in the Niger Delta are repatriated from the region. This includes 78 percent of government benefits and 80 percent of multinational oil company benefits, leaving the area with very little or nothing. Therefore, over 90 percent of the population, which includes youth and women, apart from having nothing to gain directly from the government, cannot also benefit indirectly through the marginal populations the government has been able to touch.

Arising from the above, the majority of the population the Niger Delta (youth and women who are mostly found in the informal sector and underemployment/unemployment sector), who do not, either directly or indirectly, derive benefit(s) from either the government or the multinational oil companies had since commenced various levels and forms of agitations to either let benefit holders know that they too needed some benefits or to lobby them to encourage beneficiaries to invest benefits in the domestic Niger Delta economy.

Obi (2006), highlights the reasons behind the emergence of youth restiveness thus:

> Since the late 1980s and early 1990s, there has been a renewed interest in the role of youths as social agents in Africa. Such interests developed against the background of the disruptive influence of economic crisis and structural adjustment has harsh social consequences and worsened the living conditions of vulnerable groups, including youth. With their present mired in dire straits—the retreat of the welfare state, unemployment, exploitation, suffering, hunger and anger—the youth, facing a bleak future, have reacted variously to their marginalization, alienation and dehumanization, in the quest for survival and a better future . . . the forces of resistance confront the forces of exploitation, extraction, accumulation, and repression.

This well-intentioned advocacy by youth in the Niger Delta was recently hijacked by hooligans who see the scenario as an attractive opportunity for them to make easy money. In the new technique, the youths have in many cases been involved in violent agitations: closing the worksites of multinational oil companies; kidnapping workers of multinational oil companies; killing and maiming workers of multinational oil companies and the government; and high-level piracy targeting the government, multinational oil companies, and citizens. Arising from these altercations, ransom payments by the government and multinational oil companies to these criminals provided subsistence. These payments encouraged the hitherto peaceful and focused youth advocates to join the bandwagon, as this seemed the only way they could derive monetary benefits. This increased the ranks of the violent youth agitators. In order to stop the new "commando" styled youth agitation, the government and oil companies spent colossal sums and time to fragment the youths to reduce their strength, while openly denouncing the payment of ransom to the seemingly youth and community groups.

Youths now see that violent advocacy and agitation, which results in restiveness, can bring some form of earnings from the resource pool, thus an intensification of their agitation ploys with differing and more sophisticated ideas of every instance. Youths in the Niger Delta Region, for instance, could be conservatively estimated to own and keep illegally 90 percent of arms in the region, which in many cases are used to threaten and maim for benefits from the benefit pool of government and the multinational oil companies. The proof of this assertion can be seen in the exchange of arms and ammunitions by the Niger Delta militants for the amnesty programme of the Nigerian government.

As the violent advocacy and agitation, which the youths conveniently adopted to earn some benefit from the resource pool, is seriously challenged by government, the youths see the stoppage of this great tool for benefit derivation from the region's resource pool as unthinkable. Thus, they resolve to fight with the government and multinational oil companies to maintain the status quo. The result of this has been recurring cases of restiveness of youths of the Niger Delta.

6.4 Some Petroleum Laws

Several laws operated in the petroleum industry in Nigeria have been indicated by many researchers into the root causes of restiveness in the Niger Delta.

The Environmental Rights Action (ERA) sees petroleum laws currently operating in the country as an albatross to the development of the region. They argue that a situation where a community's resources is abusively exploited, leaving the community totally vulnerable to environmental challenges without allowing the community to share in the proceeds of the benefits extracted from its belly is enough to elicit restiveness once the people are enlightened to know their rights. That in many cases their reaction to share in their resource may not be organized since the law does not allow them lawful and organized entry into the benefits from the resources derived from their environment.

It is important to note that arising from issues like this that was thrown by researchers who went to interact with the people, the federal government of Nigeria in its recent effort to overhaul of petroleum laws in Nigeria, had recommended in the Petroleum Industry Bill (PIB) it submitted to the National Assembly in 2009, that oil-producing communities should have a share of 10 percent from oil proceeds accruing to the nation. This, it is hoped, will correct earlier imbalances while encouraging people to see themselves as partners with the government and the petroleum industry in the oil business taking place in their communities. The government also sees the decision as the panacea that may radically reduce the community disturbances of oil operations in their communities, since they will now see themselves as stakeholders in the business. This means, therefore, that they will even protect the operations of the oil multinational oil companies in order for them to get their royalty and other ancillary gains.

The Land Use Reform Bill that has been submitted by the federal government to the National Assembly is in the same direction. It is also aimed at assuaging the agitations of communities arising from indiscriminate sequestering of their land holdings by government without adequate or proper input from those communities.

6.5 Inter-communal Conflicts

This factor has been commonly indicated by various studies as being a major cause of youth restiveness in the Niger Delta. In the works of Imobighe, Bassey, and Asuni (2002) on conflict and instability in the Niger Delta, they indicated pointedly that the Warri crises resulted chiefly from inter-communal conflict: the conflicts between the Ijaws and Istekeris on the one hand, and Urobho and Istekiri on the other hand. Conflicts of this nature have led to heavy militarization of the youths of these communities, who are the ones who fight in the conflicts. When the conflicts are finally contained, there are no clear plans to either demobilize the communities or make the youths voluntarily return the arms they used while in the conflict. They then use such arms to perpetuate other crimes in the community, since there are no other community wars for them to engage in.

6.6 Political Patronage

The restoration of the country's current political democracy was in the throes of the conflicts in the Niger Delta. To get support and votes from the Niger Delta communities, politicians had to play along with criminals. Some of the criminals were even engaged by politicians to force election victories for them, even while they were not needed by their people. In this case, the criminals engaged in intimidation, killing, maiming, and vote-rigging among others to sway elections in favour of their masters. Of course, to clinically undertake this assignment, they had to be properly armed by the politicians. The arms were, however, non-retrievable. The inability of the political class to retrieve the arms from the youths that supported them into power opened an opportunity for these youths to engage in illegal arms running and dealings.

6.7 Oil Bunkering

In the late 1980s, agitation for the reduction of the very obvious contrasting living conditions of oil-producing communities, *vis-à-vis* the mega oil companies' flow stations estate, had started gathering momentum. Communities in their various protests were insisting on having their communities upgraded and facilities like pipe-borne water, roads, electricity, and other infrastructure and soft items that will better their lives provided. In the absence of strong government presence at the grassroots level, the community saw the oil companies as the government. The oil companies also did not fare better, as they were entering and discussing with communities without any recourse to government, especially at the grassroots level.

The agitations, which were reminiscent of the nationalistic struggles internationally, was led by the youths and supported strongly by the elders of the various communities. In the neo-struggle, the Ogonis led the onslaught with Ken Saro Wiwa and other notable Ogoni sons and daughters anchoring with

MOSOP (Movement for the Survival of Ogoni People). The genuineness of the agitations and clarity of purpose and declarations was very obvious. In the neo-struggle era (the 1980s) communities took over the initiative to challenge the oil companies they saw to provide them with basic amenities of livelihood. At this time, the government, oil companies and community leadership did not see the emerging agitations as threat to peace. They treated this as a common issue that can always be brushed aside once it evokes. Also, as government continually did not show any interest in the lives of the Niger Delta people who were producing the oil wealth of the nation, the community leadership worsened the situation as they captured any "half-hearted" benefit intended for the community by the oil companies for themselves and close families and friends.

On the dual side of community agitations for social amenities from oil companies and government was a thriving illegal bunkering business. Although this activity was based in oil-producing communities, the content of the active participants and stakeholders were foreign. These illegal bunkerers were stealing petroleum crude from the various flow stations located in the Niger Delta communities, especially the creek communities. With the beefing up of security around oil facilities and flow stations, the illegal bunkering trade started suffering decline and recession. However, the emerging mild and sane community agitations in the oil communities provided an opportunity or sluice for the illegal bunkerers to now partner with, use, and hide under the shield of community to regain their lost trade. Also, the oil companies–induced communal crises and chieftaincy disputes provided further opportunities for the ingenious illegal bunkerers to use to their advantage.

The outside illegal bunkering elements saw the community agitations as a huge resource that will help open the access to unfettered illegal oil bunkering. For this, they encouraged communities' agitations against oil companies. Once a protest was called by an oil-producing community, their target was to encourage the communities to occupy the oil flow stations while driving the oil company workers and security away. They provided light arms for the community youths to man the flow stations while the community leadership would be calling on the companies to negotiate. While the process of negotiation was ongoing, the bunkerers, with the cover of community, collected oil illegally from the flow stations. When the community leadership, who in many cases were not part of the illegal business, saw that the bunkerers were using their genuine community agitation to perpetrate crime that was condemned by government and the oil companies, they started retreating, while blaming and condemning the act. However, the retreat and condemnation were rather late, as the youths who were recruited into this business had started deriving some financial benefits that they had never seen before, so they would never want to leave the trade, as no commensurate better legal trade was proposed by their elders, oil companies, or government. To keep the business flowing for their benefit and that of their masters, the collaborating youths were encouraged to engage and take over community leadership from elders who were not willing to accept them. This in many cases would involve armed struggle, which the bunkerers provided.

Also, the oil companies–induced community leadership and ownership tussles encouraged massive acquisition of arms and ammunitions by communities and kings for their youths to use in engaging their opponents in various degrees of warfare. With their enhanced armory sophistication and competence, the youths started dethroning kingdoms and traditional institutions while making themselves kings and community heads and leaders.

With the emerging celebration of firepower madness over knowledge, these armed criminal youths working for the bunkerers took over reign of the oil-producing communities of the Niger Delta, causing serious and various conflicts, scaring their people and oil companies away from their bases, and having a free illegal bunkering field day.

6.8 Long Period of Neglect

One of the issues that was always easily brought up in the past when discussing the Niger Delta problem is the neglect of the region by the government. Previous governments in Nigeria totally neglected the development needs of the Niger Delta people and its environment, even when the region produced the wealth of the nation. The difficult nature in accessing the region is attributed to such neglect. Infrastructures, such as roads, electricity, and pipe-borne water, which are very basic, were not provided. At a point in time, the Niger Delta people did not know government; they saw the oil companies as their government, thus heaping all their demands of provisions that would been naturally provided by the government on the oil companies. Agitations by communities for the provision of pipe-borne water, schools, medical centers, and jetties, among others, that would have been directed at the government were put on the doorsteps of the oil companies, because the oil companies were the only semblance of organized structure or government representative operating in their environment, since they could afford the travel to the cities to search for and get government attention. When oil companies delayed in addressing the needs of the communities that were not legitimately theirs, the communities started becoming restive and violent in pressing home their demands. Simple struggles like this later led to more organized riots and violence that resulted in sustained restiveness.

6.9 Destruction of Alternative Sources of Livelihood

Ashton-Jones, N., Arnott, S., and Douglas, O. (1998) and the Environmental Rights Action (2007), in their studies, strongly indicated the destruction of the environment of the Niger Delta Region as a major problem that led to the restiveness in the region. Due to oil production activities in the region, especially seismic activities and oil spills, the traditional sources of livelihood, primarily agriculturally based (farming and fishing), started becoming extinct. This condition made the predominant population of the Niger Delta, who are primarily fishermen and farmers, to be either unemployed or underemployed, brewing a situation where people were in want of livelihoods. This condition therefore raised an army of willing tools for restiveness in the region.

6.10 Non Participation of Host Communities in Economic Activities Happening in Their Communities

In the early operations of the oil multinational companies, the oil-bearing communities in which they operated in many cases never knew at all what the oil companies were doing in their communities, as they never even consulted the communities or sought to involve them in their activities once they obtained a government License to Operate (LTO). Later in the operations of these multinational oil firms, however, the firms discovered that awareness was growing in the region—not after the actions of Isaac Boro and the eye-popping revelations of Ken Saro Wiwa's MOSOP. With the increasing level of awareness, communities started agitating to be involved in the operations of the multinational oil companies. It was here that the oil companies realized that the LTO in the communities was, not only granted by the government, but also by the communities. Violence and riots ensued, giving room for restiveness as a result of the agitation of the communities to be involved in the activities of the oil firms operating in those communities.

It is in realization of this factor as a major cause of youth restiveness in the Niger Delta that the government of President Umaru Musa Yar'dua initiated the Petroleum Industry Bill (PIB), which has recommended a 10 percent royalty payment from profits oil production to the oil bearing communities. This is indicative of the fact that if communities are part owners of the oil facilities in the Niger Delta, they will be interested in protecting them.

6.11 "Aspirin Solutions" by Multinationals Operating in the Area to Buy Peace

It was interesting to note that many multinational oil companies operating in the Niger Delta Region resorted to "aspirin solutions" to buy quick in-roads and community

LTOs. The "aspirin solution" model developed by Ekong (1994) depicts a situation where one tries to, for instance, cure a terminal sickness like acute malaria, with a dose of aspirin. The model shows that the condition will improve for a little while and a terrible relapse will follow thereafter, making the effort and resources spent in acquiring the aspirin useless.

These multinational firms in order to keep the community youths at peace or at bay from coming to disrupt work on their sites pay them standby wages to stay at home. Standby Wages are wages paid to community youths to stay at home, without going to site or involving in any form of activity to either acquire skill or impart skill. The consideration here by oil firms is always that if such wage is paid, the youths who would come to their sites to create problems will be happy staying at home to enjoy their unearned income. Also, that this will reduce the total spending of theirs if they had taken the youths to site, for example, expenditures like those for healthcare, end of contract payoffs, and other sundry earnings that would have accrued to them if they had worked on site. Also, the oil firms feared a situation where the community youths will come to their sites and corrupt their real workers by encouraging them to fight for rights and union activities.

This condition led to a situation where the youths who were paid some money they never worked for started using it to acquire arms in preparation for communal crises, political thuggery activities, robbery, and pirating. When the pay is stopped at the end of contract, they now devise other means of livelihood by, in many cases, using the acquired arms for illegal business. This factor contributed seriously in fuelling youth restiveness in the Niger Delta Region.

6.12 Payment of Right of Way and Royalties

Many communal conflicts that created the conditioning leverage for youth restiveness in the Niger Delta were linked with the payment on right of way and local royalties by oil multinational oil companies to communities in the Niger Delta. This activity has caused serious divisions in the communities, leading to fractionalization and the popping up of splinter community groupings and emergence of multiple leadership lines. This situation in many cases in the Niger Delta had led to inter and intra communal wars; the result being the obvious generation and sustenance of the restive situation in the region.

Chapter 7

THE ECONOMIC BENEFIT OF YOUTH RESTIVENESS

7.1 Background

The Niger Delta Region of Nigeria has been identified as Nigeria's poorest region and most backward in terms of development. The UNDP social economic index in its 2009 report shows Nigeria as one of the poorest in the world. Compounding the poverty situation in the region are the near non-existence of power, all-season motorable link roads, potable water and health care facilities that consist the basic needs of development.

Contrastingly, the Niger Delta Region produces over 80 percent of Nigeria's wealth. The region produces the total of the oil and gas resource of Nigeria that is the main revenue earner for the country. Notwithstanding the wealth derived from the region, successive governments in Nigeria had neglected the development of the region. Rather, the Niger Delta Region had been opened to be raped, used and abandoned when their useful oil resources is depleted. The cases of Utapate oil field in Iko, Eastern Obolo Local government of Akwa Ibom Sate, and Oloibiri (the first oil community in the Niger Delta and Nigeria) in Ogbia Local Government Area of Bayelsa State explain our assertion.

The neglect of the region by successive governments midwifed a scenario where poverty, hopelessness, and illiteracy have become the major characteristics of the Niger Delta people. Since the majority of the Niger Delta populations are unable to access the wealth pool of the oil activities operating in their region, poverty becomes the order of the day. Still swimming and wallowing in their poverty and hopelessness, the youths eventually realized that they could through their restive activities earn some money from government and the oil multinational oil companies operating in their communities.

Making the situation more grim and miserable in the Niger Delta Region is the high corruption index, as reported by Transparency Initiative (an internationally recognized and respected anti-corruption monitoring group). The Organization's Annual Report in 2009 ranks Nigeria as the second most corrupt nation in the world.

Further showing disrespect and total insensitivity to the plight of the people of the area is the complete absence of infrastructure like roads or year-round access to the oil-bearing communities. Year-round motorable access roads to the oil farms located in the communities are built by the multinational oil corporation for the companies' use only. Also, in these communities where there is no electricity or good drinking-water sources, multinational oil companies' flow stations and exquisite estates (which the communities are barred from getting near) are lavished with a constant supply of electricity and potable water (the case of a dual economy). For instance, Bayelsa State was only recently in 2009 connected to the national power grid after many years of power use and utilization in Nigeria. Also, in the region, the people live in and around water so totally polluted that it has become totally injurious and unsupportive to humans and aquatic lives, due to the prospecting and production activities of multinational oil companies working in concert with the Nigerian federal government. Recall that the oil operation in Nigeria is a joint venture business between the federal government of Nigeria, represented by the Nigerian National Petroleum Corporation (NNPC), and the oil companies.

To worsen the situation, children have no access to quality education. Schools are either not there or not accessible at all, and the few ones available have no teachers or instructors. This have led to an increased level of illiteracy in the region while raising an army of easily available bunch of hungry unemployable and illiterate population, who may not be able to decipher from what is constitutionally lawful or otherwise.

Since the majority of the Niger Delta populations are unable to access the wealth pool of the oil business activities operating in their region, poverty takes over and becomes entrenched. While still wallowing in their poverty and hopelessness, the youths eventually realized that they could use restiveness as a weapon to gate-crash the wealth derived from the resources found in their soil by the multinational oil corporations and government. For instance, if youths close down a flow station and forcefully and illegally take it over while demanding social amenities from the oil companies and government, they will get immediate attention. Also, illegal buyers of crude oil will scamper to steal oil from the "flow stations" while paying less than the commensurate fee for the quantity of oil stolen to the community youths. With the realization they can earn money from illegal bunkering of crude oil in their communities, the Niger Delta youths became conscious of having within their control a weapon that, if wielded well, could redistribute income in the wide-income disparity region. This led to the entrenchment and spread of restiveness across the length and breadth of the Niger Delta Region, which resulted in an obvious sickening and negative impact on the Nigerian economy while encouraging illegality and violence across the communities of the Niger Delta Region.

7.2 Theoretical Issues

From a purely economic standpoint, the current restiveness situation in the Niger Delta cannot be said to be without some real economic benefit. Even though considered very heinous crimes, some of the activities that come with restiveness—kidnapping, piracy, armed robbery, bunkering, general violence, etc.—are seen by economists as economic activities. However, economists classify economic activities into categories of legal and illegal. People decide to pursue illegal activity, like crime—and in this case, restiveness—because of the benefit they derive from it.

Economists do not view criminals as deviants, nor do they suggest that their physiology is different from that of model citizens (Edwards, 2007). To an economist, crime is a question of labour supply. People choose to "work" in legal or illegal occupations. Following Becker's (1968) rational choice theory as recorded in Edward (2007), individuals choose crime if the marginal benefit of committing crime is greater than the marginal cost. People become criminals not because their basic motivation is different, but because their benefits and cost differ. Individuals allocate time to work, crime, and leisure to maximize their utilities. Benefits from criminal behaviour are the same as those behind everyday legitimate activities: the pursuit of pleasure, profit, gain, status, power, and for some satisfaction of rebelling against authority.

The marginal cost/marginal benefit diagram in Figure 1 (as in Edwards 2007) dearly demonstrates the economic theory of crime.

The marginal benefit curve for crime slopes downward. The criminal maximizes the net benefits from non-violent crimes at each period. The criminal essentially faces two problems:

1. Criminals will first execute the crime that they think will pay the most. The remaining opportunities provide lower returns.
2. As the supply of stolen goods increases, the prices their fences (receivers and buyers of stolen goods) are willing to pay diminish. Because the criminal faces diminishing returns for crime, the marginal benefits curve slopes downwards.

The marginal cost curve slopes upward because a person who commits more crime has to devote more resource to do so. Stealing purses or cigarettes from shops does not require as many resources as creating and organizing an international gang of shoplifters, for instance. The cost of criminal activities also results from internal and external deterrents. Internal deterrent signify the self-restraint of the person. For most people, internal deterrents are sufficient to make crime a passing temptation.

External deterrents are calculated by estimating the probabilities of getting caught, convicted, or sentenced

(Edwards, 2007). For most people, jail time will carry an extra cost of embarrassment and a decreased probability of finding a comparable job and even a respectable place to live afterward. These advantages force the criminal into the underground economy once the sentence is finished. But for others, jail time may provide rights and respect. In addition, while in prison, they have the chance to network with others of their "profession" and perfect their skills. The result for both of these groups is a high recidivism rate (the rate at which criminals are convicted again) (Deutsch, Hakim, Spiegel, 1990; CBSNews.com, 2004). In Nigeria, experience shows that some criminals see prisons as a comfortable abode and home that they do not have or can afford outside. Many prison-returning criminals insist that they are more sure of constant food in prison than outside, thus deciding to remain jailbirds.

Fig. 7.1 Marginal Cost/Benefit of Crime

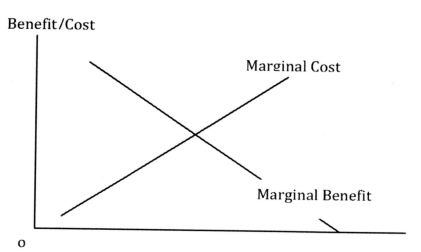

7.3 Restiveness as a Resource for Redistributing Income

7.3.1 Is There Income Inequality in the Niger Delta Region?

Over the years, Nigeria and indeed other developing countries have been classified by development economist and economics historian as countries caught in the web of high income disparity. Although a very rich country, owing to the revenue she derives from the sales, of crude oil and other petroleum products (the main income earner of the country), the income and wealth created there from has been confirmed to be in the hands of a very few in the population. This distribution has been strongly argued for by economists as being the main reason for high poverty in the country. It has a lack of basic infrastructure and public goods. The high level of poverty and lack of infrastructure coupled with high level of unemployment has in recent history forced the teeming unemployed population to scamper to support themselves with illegal or legal activities. From the submission of economists on Nigeria as shown above, it can be confirmed that there is an income equality gap in the country. A gloomy picture of the socio-economic condition of the Niger Delta occasioned by the income disparity-induced poverty is shown in table 7.1.

Table 7.1 shows that the huge earnings of the Niger Delta states from oil revenue are not optimally utilized to solve the problems of development in the region by the government. Life expectancy is averaged at 0.50 for the region. It could be noticed that life expectancy index performance of the state defies the earnings structure of the states from oil

Table 7.1 Human Development Index (HDI) for the Delta States, 2005

S/N	State	Life Expectancy	Education Index	GDP Index	HDI
1	Abia	0.492	0.578	0.560	0.543
2	Akwa Ibom	0.506	0.683	0.540	0.576
3	Bayelsa	0.455	0.523	0.520	0.499
4	Cross River	0.556	0.630	0.565	0.584
5	Delta	0.578	0.636	0.621	0.615
6	Edo	0.597	0.602	0.600	0.594
7	Imo	0.503	0.546	0.591	0.547
8	Ondo	0.501	0.575	0.512	0.529
9	Rivers	0.563	0.590	0.620	0.591

Source: Environmental Resource and Management Ltd Field Survey (2005), in Akpan (2011)

revenue. Cross River State, for instance, collects the least revenue of the entire core Niger Delta states yet has a higher life expectancy index than states like Akwa Iborn, Bayelsa, Ondo, Abia, Ondo, and Imo. Similar trends can also be seen in the other variables in terms of states' performance. This is indicative of the fact that oil earning does not translate directly into development or improvement in the Niger Delta Region. Therefore, good governance and not necessarily oil revenue earnings could bring desired positive change in the Niger Delta Region.

7.3.1 Theoretical Concepts on Inequality

7.3.1.1 *The Lorenz Curve*

Income inequality so identified above can be measured in several ways. The most widely used graphical method depicts a Lorenz Curve. The Lorenz Curve measures the cumulative proportion (between 0 and 100 percent of the population) on the horizontal axis and a cumulative measure of income or wealth (0 percent to 100 percent) on the vertical axis. Fig. 7.2 shows three Lorenz Curves. The 45 line shows an economy with perfect income equality; for example, 10 percent of the population has 10 percent of the cc income. Everyone in this economy has the same income. The second extreme case is the "backward L" that constitutes the base and the right axis of the diagram. This curve shows an almost total inequality. About 99.9 percent of the population has no income, while about 0.01 percent has it all. Finally, the "middle" Lorenz curve shows a reality common to many regions. For example, in the United States in 2002, the lowest quintile of households had 3.4 percent of the total income; the two lowest quintiles 12.2 percent and the three lowest quintiles 27.1 percent. Meanwhile, the lowest 80 percent of the households earned 50.3 percent, leaving 49.7 percent of the aggregate household income of the United States for the top quintile (De Navas-Walt, Cleveland, and Webster, 2003).

7.3.1.2 *Gini Coefficient*

Another key instrument for measuring the extent to which the income distribution differs from 45° line is the Gini Coefficient. The Gini Coefficient is derived from the Lorenz Curve. A Gini Coefficient for the middle Lorenz Curve in Fig 7.2 is G= A/A+B, where A is the area between the line

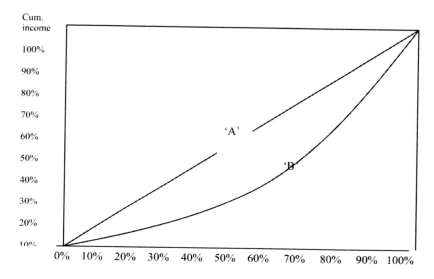

(Cumulative Proportion of Population)

of perfect equality and the Lorenz Curve itself. A represents the area below the Lorenz Curve but above the curve of completed inequality. The Gini Coefficient takes on a value between 0 and 1. The more equal the income distribution, the closer is area A to 0 and the smaller the Gini Coefficient. The Gini Coefficient equals 0 for the curve of perfect equality (because A = 0). Alternatively, the Gini Coefficient equals 1 in the case of complete inequality (because B = 0).

The Gini Coefficient is a measure of statistical dispersion development by the Italian statistician Corrado Gini and published in his 1912 paper "Variability and Mutability." The Gini Coefficient is a measure of the inequality of a distribution, a value of 0 expressing total equality and value of 1 maximal inequality. It has found application in the study of inequalities in disciplines as diverse as diverse as economics, health science, ecology, chemistry, and engineering. It is commonly used as a measure of inequality of income or wealth, worldwide. Gini coefficients for income range from approximately 0.23 (Sweden) to 0.70 (Namibia) although not every country has been assessed (Wikipedia, 2012). The Gini coefficient is usually defined mathematically based on the Lorenz Curve, which plots the proportion of the total income of the population (y-axis) that is cumulatively earned by the bottom X axis (percent) of the population (Fig. 7.2).

Some find it more intuitive (and it is mathematically equivalent) to think of the Gini Coefficient as half of the relative mean difference. The mean difference is the average absolute difference between two items selected randomly from a population, ant the relative mean difference is the mean difference divided by the average, to normalize for scale.

If the Gini Coefficient is investigated for the Niger Delta, especially prior to the zenith of youth restiveness in the region, the prediction will obviously be a figure close to 1 or complete inequality. However, the Gini index for Nigeria in 2008 was put at 43.7 percent or 0.44 in the scale of 0 to 1 adopted in this text.

7.3.2 Activities of Niger Delta Youths that Redistribute Income

As earlier explained, the particular activities that come with youth restiveness in the Niger Delta Region include kidnapping, piracy, bunkering, armed robbery, and political thuggery. From these activities, the youths derive income. However, such income is considered illegal and is not included in the country's GNP or GDP.

With the increased tempo of the illegal activities by the youths of the Niger Delta, encapsulated in the restiveness condition, a lot of illegal income was earned by the youths. For instance, in 2009, the Nigerian National Petroleum Corporation (NNPC) announced that it spent a whopping $12 million dollars to buy peace to operate (essentially, an LTO) in the Nigeria Delta region. This payment was reportedly made to the various groups and gangs of youths operating in the Niger Delta Region. The youths also made a lot of money from kidnapping and piracy. The Niger Delta Region has been internationally reputed recently as a very high risk area for kidnapping and hostage taking, and the Gulf of Guinea, which bounds the region, has been internationally reported to be the second most dangerous marine route in the world after Somalia's Gulf of Aden, where daredevil sea pirates operate. A BBC report in January 2010 describes Niger Delta pirates as those who, after robbing their prey, take delight in killing them, in total contrast to the Somali pirates whose interest is only to collect ransom.

It is thus obvious that the restive activities of the youths in the Nigeria Delta region have created an economic corridor for them to make money. Since the money here is made from other wealth holders like multinational corporations, rich citizens, local governments, state governments, and the federal government (stealing of the country's crude oil resources through illegal bunkering), the assertion of wealth redistribution as a result of youth restiveness in the Niger Delta thus becomes very tenable, true, and arguable.

7.4 Economic Value of Youth Restiveness

In a strict economic sense of reasoning and analysis, a closer view of youth restiveness in the Niger Delta will lead to identifying the immense economic benefits that have accrued from this situation. If we consider and even disaggregate the various activities involved in youth restiveness, we can easily identify where some economic benefits were being earned either by the youths, the community, the oil companies, or government.

However, before we sojourn into a detailed analysis of the economic benefits derivable from youth restiveness, it is proper we show the physical manifestation of restiveness as mostly witnessed in the Niger Delta. Aside from the riotous and violent strategies that coloured the restive situation when it started initially, a more sophisticated and less risky way, garnished with emerging technology, has been recently adopted and made so popular that it not only enveloped the character of youth restiveness in the Niger Delta Region but has slowly been outsourced to other regions of Nigeria. The new and more desirable strategy in the restiveness tools kit is now kidnapping. The Niger Delta youth maybe embrace kidnapping because it is cost effective and easier to execute with fewer casualties and a lower operational cost than other crime types. Proceeds are also more predictable, as ransom is decided during pre-operations.

7.4.1 KIDNAPPING OR HOSTAGE TAKING IN THE NIGER DELTA

Table 7.2 shows a list of some hostage taking or kidnappings carried out by armed militant youths in the Nigeria Delta that obviously fueled the youth restiveness in the region. Although government and the international community has taken a stand against the payment of ransom for kidnapping in the Niger Delta or elsewhere in the world, it is widely believed that ransom was paid for all cases reported either by the employer(s) of the kidnapped, or families of the kidnapped, and even in some cases the government had been fingered.

Table 7.2 List of Some Hostage Taking in Oil Rich Niger Delta, Nigeria (Updated 29th January, 2008).

S/N	Month/ Year	State incident Occurred	No of Hostage Victims	Place Of Hostage Taking	Parent/ Subsidiary
1	Oct 2006	AKWA-IBOM	8	Near Eket	Bristol Helicopters Company
2	3rd June 2007		7 (one killed)	Ikot-Abasi	Aluminum smelter Coy of Nigeria
3	2003	BAYELSA	18	Middleton and Pennington offshore platform	Chevron Texaco
4	Dec 2004		1	Ekeremor	SPDC
5	10th Jan 2004		4	Offshore EA oil platform	SPDC
6	July 2001		4	Ekeremor LGA	Trico Supply Coy Norwegian Shipping Firm

(Continued)

S/N	Month/ Year	State incident Occurred	No of Hostage Victims	Place Of Hostage Taking	Parent/ Subsidiary
7	Jun 2006		1	Gbarain near Yenagoa	Westminster dredging (International)
10	Nov 2006		2	Bilabiri	Norwegian Oil Service Coy
11	7th Dec 2006		4	Twon-brass (Termial)	Agip (NAOC)
12	10th Jan 2007		9	Ogu-Yenagoa	Daewoo Nig. Ltd
13	24th Jan 2007		9	Sagbama	Chinese National Petroleum Corp. (CNPC)
14	March 2007		2	Bayelsa	SETRACO NIG. LTD
15	March 2007		3	Koluama 1	EBEOBI NIG. LTD
16	1st May 2007		6	Funiwa Oil field	Chevron Nig. Ltd
17	5th May, 2007		10	Sangan-AKASSA	Conoil

(Continued)

S/N	Month/ Year	State incident Occurred	No of Hostage Victims	Place Of Hostage Taking	Parent/ Subsidiary
18	June 2007		26 (including Soldiers & Agip workers)	Ogboinbiri	Nigeria Army & Agip (NAOC)
19	June 2007		1 (over 70 yr woman)	Akaibiri, Yenagoa	Mother of Bayelsa State, Speaker
20	1st July 2007		1 (over 2 yr old child)	Yenagoa	Son of Governor's Office Staff
28	Dec 2007	BAYELSA	1 (91 yr old man)	Bolou-orua, Sagbama L.G.A.	Father of the Accountant General of Bayelsa State
29	1999	RIVERS	Aleibiri, Ekeremor L.G.A	When flow station (Ahoada West)	Helicopter pilots
30	1999	1	1	Ebeolom-Abua	JN/A
32	2005		1	Mbiama	Daewoo Nig. Ltd
33	2006		2	Port Harcourt	Daewoo Nig. Ltd

(Continued)

S/N	Month/ Year	State incident Occurred	No of Hostage Victims	Place Of Hostage Taking	Parent/ Subsidiary
34	11th May 2006		3		Saipem (Agrip Contractor)
35	10th June 2006		2	Port Harcourt	Beaufort International
36	July 2006		1	Port Harcourt	Bilfinger Berger (B+B)
37	4th Aug 2006		3	Port Harcourt	N/A
38	19th Aug 2006		4	Port Harcourt	International Dredging coy.
39	Aug 2006		2	Port Harcourt	B+B
40	13th Aug 2006		4	Port Harcourt	N/A
41	16th Aug 2006		1	Port Harcourt	Saipem
42	24th Aug 2006		1	Port Harcourt	SPDC-Contract Firm

(Continued)

S/N	Month/ Year	State incident Occurred	No of Hostage Victims	Place Of Hostage Taking	Parent/ Subsidiary
43	Oct 2006		25	Cawthome channel	Eni SPA subsidiary of Agrip Oil Co
44	22nd Nov 2006		7	50 Km off Coast off Rivers State	Sichuan Tele-comm. Coy
45	Jan 2007		5	Emohua, River State	Nigerian Navy Officers
46	Jan 2007		2	River State	
47	Jan 2007		2	Port Harcourt	Pivot G. I. S Coy
51	18th Feb 2007		3	Port Harcourt	Hydro Dive Coy
52	March 2007		1	Port Harcourt	Julius Berger plc.
53	30th April 2007	1	1	Ubima, Rivers State	Gov. Celestine Omehia Mother
54	2nd May 2007	1	11	Ayama, Rivers State	Daewoo Engineering & construction coy

(Continued)

S/N	Month/ Year	State incident Occurred	No of Hostage Victims	Place Of Hostage Taking	Parent/ Subsidiary
55	May 2007	.	6	55 miles off the coast of river State	Eni SPA
56	5th May, 2007		1	Port Harcourt	Belarusian Woman, wife of Nigeria-Akwa Ibom State
57	19th May 2007		2	Port Harcourt	Petro-chemicals firm
61	June 2007		3 yr old child (master St. Michael Steward	Port Harcourt	In a private Nursery School
62	4th June 2007		5 (2 Nigerian & 3 foreigners)	Soku, Rivers State	SPDC
63	5th June 2007		3 yrs old British Magaret hills	Port Harcourt	Briton
64	8th July 2007		2 Nigerians	Near Buguma. River State	SPDC Contractors

(Continued)

108

S/N	Month/ Year	State incident Occurred	No of Hostage Victims	Place Of Hostage Taking	Parent/ Subsidiary
65	12th July 2007		3 yr old Nigerian child (Prince Samuel Amadi)	East-West Road, Port Harcourt	Ikwerre Community (son of a royal Highness)
66	Aug 2007		2	Port Harcourt	Engineering firm staff
67	Aug 2007		2	Port Harcourt	ADC Engineering firm Mtn)
68	Aug 2007		1	Port Harcourt	Hydro dive Company
69	Sept 2007		1 (Solito Bareba)	Woji-P.H	Fresh Graduate
80	8th May 2007		4	Okan Oil Feild	Global offshore (Chevron Nig. Ltd.)
81	May 2007		1	Enerhen Junction, Warri	

Source: *Niger Delta Development Monitoring and Corporate Watch,* (NID–DEMCOW), *a Non-governmental Organization, based in Bayelsa State, Nigeria. Nengi James (MR.), Executive Director.*

According to the Niger Delta Development Monitoring and Corporate Watch (NID-DEMCOW), in an email sent to some media houses, between 1999 and June 2007, 50 cases of hostage takings and kidnappings have been reported in the oil-rich Niger Delta. Of course, this excludes the chilling incidents in July 2007 when children were also kidnapped, ostensibly, for ransom. Among such was the kidnapping of a three-year-old British girl in Port Harcourt, Rivers State on her way to school. The case attracted international attention and was carried live as breaking news by such media organization as BBC, CNN, and Sky News.

In the eighty-one cases documented by NDDEMCOW, an NGO based in Bayelsa, in Table 7.3, a total of 346 hostages were reportedly taken. The breakdown shows that of that number, 15 were held in Akwa Ibom, 147 in Bayelsa State, and 139 in Rivers State. If we were to consider cases or reported ransom payment made to kidnappers in recent times in the oil rich Niger Delta between 2006 and 2008, the peak and frightening period of the kidnapping or hostage taking crises in the Niger Delta, we can therefore conservatively assume an average ransom payment of 10 million naira per kidnapped person. Keeping this assumption, it could be estimated that for 346 persons kidnapped or taken hostage as in Table 7.2, over 3 billion naira was paid to the kidnappers as ransom.

Table 7.3 also records hostage taking in the Niger Delta Region between 2006 and 2008. This data published by Environmental Watch (NGO based in Port Harcourt, 2008), lists the activities of Niger Delta militants, different from the general picture shown in table 7.2 that is richly inclusive of the hostage taking activities of criminal elements within the struggle. This records forty-four hostage-taking incidents spread across the states of the Niger Delta. The picture here depicts the peak period of the activities of the Niger Delta militants and majority of the attacks were on the oil multinational oil companies and security agents. No attack here was targeted at individuals or other group in the Niger delta outside oil-related and government interests. The seriousness of the Niger Delta militants in their freedom and redemption fight and struggle was brought to the fore when they attacked the Shell Petroleum Development Company facility in Port Harcourt, River State, killing seventeen Nigerian soldiers on the 15th of January. On 2nd October 2006, ten Nigerian soldiers were killed by militant Niger Delta youths. Two days after, 4th October 2006, nine soldiers were killed by Niger Delta militant youths. Another soldier was killed on 22nd November 2006 by Niger Delta militant youths. The series of killings of Nigerian military personnel persisted until 2008, as shown in Table 7.3. These actions were intended to send a message to the federal government of Nigeria that the young militants were ready to sustain the struggle to control their resources.

Apart from attacking and killing government security operatives, Table 7.3 shows varied attacks on oil installations and the taking into hostage of oil company workers-mostly expatriates. An interesting and intriguing issue was when militant youths, on the 16th of May 2007, attacked the country home of the Vice President of Nigeria, Dr. Goodluck Ebele Jonathan, who is the current President of the Federal Republic of Nigeria and an indigent of the Niger Delta.

Table 7.3 Cases of Hostage Taking in the Niger Delta Region

S/N	Date	Incident	Where	Casualty	Loss
1	11/01/06	Unidentified gun men carried attack on Royal Dutch/Shell's facility	Offshore EA Field, River State	4 foreign oil workers kidnapped	120,000 bpd
2	11/1/2006	Explosion on major crude oil pipeline operated by Royal Dutch/shell	Forcados,		100,000 bpd
3	15/01/06	Royal Dutch / Shell facility attacked by MEND fighters	Port Harcourt, Rivers State	17 soldiers were killed. Unknown numbers of militants and shell's employees also died	
4	10/1/2006	Executive with US based Baker Hughes was shot and killed.	Port Harcourt, Rivers State	1 death	
5	2/6/2006	A Norwegian offshore rig was attacked	Port Harcourt, Rivers State	16 crew members were kidnapped	

S/N	Date	Incident	Where	Casualty	Loss
6	23/08/06	Clash between MEND and security agencies	Bayelsa	10 Mend fighters killed	
7	12/10/2006	Militants attacked chevron offshore field	Delta	1 worker killed	
8	2/10/2006	10 Nigerian soldiers were killed offshore field		10 soldiers killed	
9	3/10/2006	Western oil workers taken hostage	Bayelsa	7 western oil workers taken hostage	
10	4/10/2006	9 Nigerian soldiers were killed when they stormed a militant camp	Rivers	9 soldiers killed	
11	22/11/06	Clash between Nigerian and militants when soldiers stormed a militant camp to rescue kidnapped	Rivers	1 soldier killed	
12	7/12/2006	Kidnap of foreign oil worker	Delta	4 foreine oil worker kidnapped	

(Continued)

S/N	Date	Incident	Where	Casualty	Loss
13	21/12/06	Obagi pumping station attacked	Bonny Island, River	3 guards killed	
14	16/01/07	Militants attacked an oil vessel near Bonny Island	Funiwa		187,000 bpd
15	4/3/2007	Major spill at a pipeline feeding the Bonny export terminal due to sabotage	Rivers		150,000 bpd
16	1/5/2007	Six Expatriate worker from onshore facility owned by chevron were seized	Funiwa		150,000 bpd
17	3/5/2007	Mend seized eight foreign workers from an offshore vessel	Rivers	8 foreign workers kidnapped	50,000 bpd
18	4/5/2007	Saipem was attacked causing shut-ins production	Okono/ Okpoh, Rivers	Several oil Workers wounded	42,000 bpd

S/N	Date	Incident	Where	Casualty	Loss
19	7/5/2007	Protests caused chevron to shut down the Abiteye flow station that feeds Escrvos export terminal	Abiteye, Delta		98,000 bpd,
20	8/5/2007	Three major oil pipelines (one in Brass and two in the Akasa area) run by Agip were attacked	Brass/ Akasa, Bayelsa		170,000 bpd
21	10/5/2007	Protesters occupied the Bornu pipeline system causing shell to shut-in production feeding the Bonny light export terminal	Bornu, Rivers		
22	16/05/07	Gunmen attacked the country home of the Vice president	Ogbia, Bayelsa		77,000
31	31/10/07	MEND attacked Naval officer	Rivers	1 naval officer killed	

(Continued)

S/N	Date	Incident	Where	Casualty	Loss
32	12/11/2007	Niger delta militants		A pregnant woman allegedly killed, while 25 persons injured	
33	15/11/07	Mend attacked shell facility	Rivers State		
38	3/2/2008	MEND fighters attacked a military houseboat stationed at the shell petroleum TARA manifold	Shell petroleum TARA manifold, Bayelsa State	1 killed	
39	11/2/2008	Gunmen attacked a supply vessel belonging to Total Oil Nig. Ltd. MV Patience at Buoy 35	Kalaibama channel, Bonny Island	2 soldiers killed	

S/N	Date	Incident	Where	Casualty	Loss
40	11/2/2008	Millitant attacked a Naval gunboat belonging to the Pathfinder Naval command of Nigerian Navy escorting NLNG boats from Port Harcourt to Bonny	Rivers State	4 people killed	
41	19/03/08	Exchange of fires between militants on oil industry security ship	Rivers State		
42	21/03/08	MEND attacked naval causing explosion	Rivers State		
43	2/4/2008	Two oil flow stations belonging to Agip Oil company located offshore Forcados were blown off	Rivers State	11 soldiers reportedly killed	120,000 bpd
44	13/04/08	Agip vessels bombed	Forcados, Delta	10 Naval officers died and some militants	

Source: Environmental Watch, Port Harcourt, 2008

7.4.2 Hostage Taking with Particular View on Akwa Ibom State

Our decision to particularly single Akwa Ibom State out for treatment in this text on hostage taking is as a result of the fact that this state at the peak of restiveness crises in the Niger Delta Region remained peaceful, with oil production activities going on smoothly without stoppages and general youth restiveness remaining at near zero. Notwithstanding the rich oil potentials of the other state and the prevalence of similar restiveness-causative factors as in the other states of the region, the youths in Akwa Ibom State were generally passive to the tempting conditions of restiveness. Many studies on the Niger Delta on peace building and conflict resolution kept Akwa Ibom State as a control group. The control in many cases was to help researchers discover what factors could have made the youths of a segment of a turbulent region to remain very peaceful and in some cases passive.

The data for kidnapping in Akwa Ibom State in table 7.4 shows that between 2006 and 2010, recorded kidnapping cases stood at ninety. In 2006, only one kidnap case was recorded in Akwa Ibom State. However, the years 2006 to 2008 were the peak period of kidnapping in the Niger Delta, where other Niger Delta states (Rivers, Bayelsa, and Delta) recorded robust degree of kidnapping incidences, as shown in tables 7.2 and 7.3. This scenario indicates that Akwa Ibom State was relatively peaceful and stable, with good policies that could have contributed significantly in stemming the migration effect of kidnapping to its domain, even when the restiveness activities were very significant in the neighbouring states around her. A breakdown in the efficacy of kidnap-insulating policies in Akwa Ibom State could be noticed from 2008. Recorded incidence of kidnapping in 2008 grew from one incident recorded in 2007 to nine in 2008. To rescue the kidnap victims, colossal sums of money were spent as ransom payment to the kidnappers by victims and the government, as recorded in some known cases in the table.

In 2009, the number kidnapped in Akwa Ibom State increased to forty-eight, meaning that four persons were kidnapped per month. With this realization by the criminal kidnapping youth gangs in Akwa Ibom State that they could make a good fortune with kidnapping, they deepened their activities in this new business venture, indicated by the growth in activities in the sector. This was even as the state government had enacted a law to punish convicted kidnappers through capital punishment. This severe punishment did not, however, deter the kidnappers from stepping up their activities. Recall the theoretical underpinning of the text that criminals are enticed more into crime by the returns on such activities: that they will not mind undertaking heavy costs to get higher returns on their investment.

The booming kidnapping business in Akwa Ibom State continued into 2010, with thirty-two kidnapping cases recorded as of the second quarter of the year: meaning an average of eight kidnappings per month; a whopping 100 percent increase from the position or situation of 2009. Contrastingly, the kidnapping boom in Akwa Ibom State came when such activities had drastically reduced in the kidnapping–prone areas of her neighbouring core oil-producing Niger Delta states (Rivers, Bayelsa, and Delta). Some schools of thoughts on the Akwa Ibom State kidnapping scenario converge their description on the kidnapping causatives factors on a two situational realities model:

1. The increasing revenue earnings of Akwa Ibom State from the Federation Accounts as a result of stable oil production and the abrogation of the on-shore/offshore oil dichotomy has attracted both positive and negative economic agents to the state.

2. A possible boom in economic activities in the state, which have led to unexpected migration of the illegal economic agents (kidnappers) from neighbouring states who have come to foist their operational modus on Akwa Ibom State that did not expect such surge in the activities of these kidnappers in their domain. This text sees these two views as contributing positively and significantly to the current restiveness situation in Akwa Ibom State.

The interesting economic scenario noticed here is the colossal amount of financial resources paid out by both households and government as ransom to the kidnappers. The contention by many analysts on the emerging Akwa Ibom State kidnapping scenario had been that if the right policies and actions were taken by the security agencies and the public, the new kidnapping trade, where substantial funds were paid into illegal kidnapping market (some of which were borrowed by the households, thus committing them into indebtedness and poverty) were injected into the economy of the state, it would have positively and significantly changed the current poor status of the economy of the state. Yes, if such funds had found its way into legal economic activities in the state economy, it would have impacted on the economy positively. Any such legal investment of the ransom into the economy, even in the informal sector, would have created employment for the teeming unemployed youths who are growing into the harrowing business of kidnapping.

On the argument that earlier state government policies and in fact the present state government policies were and are not robust enough to sustain a kidnap and crime-free economy, this text rather reasons otherwise. With the rising global levels of unemployment in the country, which as of 2008 stood at about 15 percent, and with the propensity to rise further, and with inflation also rising in similar directions, there is real pressure exerted on the economy for legal means of survival that may not be available for the waiting population—thus forcing the remnant population to search for illegal means of survival in a capitalist economy like ours that does not provided for the welfare of the masses. This scenario was entangled with rising level of income inequality, with the middle-income group or bracket gradually disappearing, and the clear emergence of a dual economy. Such an economic scenario will only bring to the fore issues of survival. Given that the region had already been infested with an illegal trade for an economy that is booming, the propensity for it to spread can therefore become very strong.

7.4.3 Restiveness as a Tool for Re-distributing Wealth

From the benefits distribution chain discussed in Chapter 6, one can observe, according to the analysis there, that

Table 7.4 Kidnapping in Akwa Ibom State

S/N	Date	Names	Number kidnapped	Ransom paid
1	2008	Stemco Expatriate	1	N5m
2	2008	Ubong Obot	1	
4	2009	Mustag Ahmad	1	
5	2006	Exxon-Mobile expatriates	3	N60m
6	2009	Sen. Alloy Etuk's Wife	1	
7	2009	Nelson Effion	1	N10m
8	2009	Ita Okon Enyong (Enta-co)	1	N10m
9	2009	Apostle Okuyak Uwah	1	N5m
10	2009	Nse Ntuen	1	N50m
11	2009	Pa Kevin Edet	1	
12	2009	Mrs. Michael Bush	1	N3m
13	2009	HOP, Nsit ubium	1	N10m (killed)
14	2009	Opolopum Ette's wife	1	
15	2009	Russians (Rusal)	2	
16	2007	Russians (Rusal)	6	
17	2009	Aniefon Aniediabasi	1	
18	2009	Mrs. Iniobong Ekpenyong	1	
19	2008	StemcoStaff	6	
20	2009	Uwemedimo Archibong	1	
21	2009	Mrs. Adariana Uko	1	
22	2009	Mrs. Anne Enoidem	1	

(Continued)

S/N	Date	Names	Number kidnapped	Ransom paid
23	2009	Dr. Owen	1	
36	2009	Ediomo Udoko		
37	2009	Iniobong Sunny Jackson		
43	2009	Michael Nkono	1	
50	2009	Miss Edikan udo	1	
51	2009	Mr. Ita Enyong	1	
52	2010	Mr. John Akpan	1	
53	2010	Paramount Ruler-Okobo	1	
54	2010	Prof. Akaninyene Mendie	1	
55	2010	Clan Head of Inen Chief Obosi	1	
56	2010	Prophetess Mercy Inyang	1	
57	2010	Prophetess Mercy Effiong	1	
58	2010	Okon Effiong Mkpong	1	
59	2010	Chief Inyang Eno	1	
60	2010	Mrs. Elizabeth Phillips	1	
61	2010	Mrs. Godwin Udoaka (First Bank)	1	
62	2010	Mrs. Godwin Bassey Eton	1	
63	2010	Prof. Imoh Ukpong	1	
64	2010	Dr. Austin Edet	1	Killed
65	2010	Chief Emmanuel Etukidem	1	

(Continued)

S/N	Date	Names	Number kidnapped	Ransom paid
66	2010	Samuel Inyang (PDP, Ini LGA)	1	
67	2010	83 yr old rtd. civil servant, Mbiabong, Ikpe Annang	1	
68	2010	Mrs Rosey Jack Udota	1	
69	2010	Joel Francis (Gov. Driver)		
70	2010	Anthony Akpanobong	1	
71	2010	Barr. Archibong's wife	1	
72	2010	Stemco employees	4	
73	2010	Rev. Ntia Ntia	1	
74	2010	Deacon Sandy Ntuenibok	1	
75	2010	Rev. Ime Uyire	1	
76	2010	A female member of Rev. Ime Uyire	1	
77	2010	Mrs. Iwakkeowo Bassey Essien	1	
78	2009	Obong Mike Ene	1	
79	2008	Mr Essien Ewoh	1	
80	2010	Late Ntia's children	2	
81	2010	Dr. Uwah	1	
82	2010	Mrs Udonwa	1	Killed
83	2009	Bishop Okon Enyong	1	N12m
84	2009	Barr.Imo Udonwa	1	Killed

(*Continued*)

S/N	Date	Names	Number kidnapped	Ransom paid
85	2009	Engr. Emmanuel EKpeyong	1	Killed
86		Mathais Ekpeyong	1	Killed
87	2009	Barr. Benjamin Udoekpo	1	Killed
88		Maria Ikpe	1	Killed
89	2009	Chief paul Inyang	1	Killed
90	2010	Daughter of Local Govt. Chairman, Abak	1	Killed
91	2010	Ezekiel Peter Ebiere	1	Killed
92	2008	CCECC Expatriates	3	N60m

Source:
1. *Global Concord Newspaper-Tuesday 7th Sept, 2010.*
2. *Akwa Ibom State Police Headquarters, Uyo.*
3. *Information on ransom sourced from fieldwork survey of victims' families and close associates.*

the groups with the least or no benefits from either the government or the multinational oil firms were the groups that had the majority of youths, women and children in the communities. This skewed distribution chain created a situation in the communities where these groups were obviously impoverished. Such impoverishment could be indicated in the performance of the basic development index like access to education, access to good drinking water, access to balanced diet, access to basic health care, access to information, among others, which had been variously reported as performing very lowly in the Niger Delta (UNDP

Country Report 2008; National Bureau of Statistics 2009; and Environmental Right Action (ERA), 2008, among others).

Restiveness in the Niger Delta led to a situation where people, companies, and other interests had their arms twisted by restive youths to part with money illegally as ransoms to set free their kidnapped ones. In some cases, lives were lost in the process. In the case of closure of flow stations, the youths were paid ransom to vacate these flow stations while in many cases communities used the situation to canvass for community projects. The undertaking of such community projects helped in providing some form of employment and income to youths and women in the community (mostly those in the informal sector). This situation made the other sectors of the Niger Delta community that were not benefiting from the resources pool of its environment to also benefit, indicating some real form of income redistribution—money transferred from the exclusive control of businesses and community leaders to reach the other sectors that hitherto had no significant share in the wealth.

7.4.4 Improvement of the Socio-economic Conditions of the People

Over the period of intense youth restiveness activities in the Niger Delta, there was some remarkable improvement in the socio-economic indicators of the region. The significance of such improved socio-economic status could be easily noticed in education, hygiene, a better and more regular food supply, increased attendance and patronage of hospitals for health needs, and the creation of a more robust business environment.

The logical explanation for this could be demonstrated thus: In a community of about five thousand people (typical of most Niger Delta communities) spread over about five hundred households (using the UN standard for sub-Saharan Africa of ten people per household), if two members of each household are involved in restiveness, as explained in this text by kidnapping, armed robbery, illegal, bunkering, political thuggery, among others, each household in that community would have raised new breadwinners. Consequently, the total household earnings (legal and illegal) must have increased, perhaps enough to provide what they hitherto could not afford for their households. From the authors' experience, most of such socio-economic needs in a typical Niger Delta community include school fees and other school requirements, health services, environmental issues, hygiene, and good accommodations, among others.

In the years where restiveness thrived in the Niger Delta Region, many states of the Niger Delta disclosed improvement in their socio-economic indicators. The following conditions were noticed: improved school enrollment, increased use of hospitals, reduction in malnutrition, reduction in child mortality rate, reduction in child malnourishment rate, and improved hygiene resulting from the use of modern sewage disposal system. The remarkable improvement of the performance of these indicators could be explained by revenue into the community from the activities of restiveness. The income earning restive youths started providing comfortable houses for their families, modern toilet facilities, and school fees for siblings and children, among other provisions.

The spending of these youths in the communities created a boom and some commercial centres in these communities. The boom created avenues for employment and markets for the community entrepreneurs like liquor sellers, clothing and fashion dealers, hairdressers, barbers, local mechanics and artisans, video film sellers, patent medicine dealers, churches, motorcycle-riding thugs, and mercenaries, among others. Below is the performance of the socio-economic indicators in the Niger Delta resulting from increased restive activities in the Niger Delta Region.

7.4.4.1 Education

Proceeds made by the restive youth from bunkering, kidnapping, political thuggery, and looting oil installations, among others, have helped exceedingly in improving the general well-being of members of the perpetrators families. In the case of education, the restive youths who have families will want to use the proceeds made on their children's or siblings' education, in order to improve the quality of educational opportunities for their family members and prepare them for the "rainy day" when the youths are out of the business that brings such unearned income.

7.4.4.2 Hygiene

Another area of improved quality of life had been that of hygiene. Every development Report on the Niger Delta Region had always shown a region living in squalor and slums, where the level of hygiene was far below international and national standards. With the creation of new wealth holdings in the region, we have witnessed a situation where there were improved toilet facilities in the Niger Delta—water system toilets have been installed for use by families, eliminating the need to defecate into rivers, streams, and nearby bushes.

7.4.4.3 Food Supply

Having a balanced diet and three square meals in a day had always been a problem, creating situations of malnutrition and starvation in households in the region. The food supply chain in the Niger Delta had been noted by many studies and reports as being very inadequate. With the advent of new wealth holdings created by the restive youths from unearned sources, the food supply to families and households improved tremendously. For new children born into the region, the hope of survival is not all lost.

7.4.4.4 Improved Health Care

As more community people earn more income, either legally or illegally, there is a tendency for people to seek orthodox medical facilities to attend to their health problems. Increased patronage of orthodox medical facilities therefore reduces health concerns and infant mortality, increases life expectancy, and reduces maternal deaths in communities in the region.

7.4.4.5 Creation of a Robust Business Environment

The eventual flow of unearned income into the region from restiveness led to the emergence of a burgeoning local economy in the communities. Since in many cases; the kidnappers rarely leave the communities for fear of being arrested or killed by government law enforcements agents, they remain in the communities and spend their monies there. This condition therefore generates a growing economy, and, in many cases, creates employment and other economic and social opportunities.

Chapter 8

THE ECONOMIC CONSEQUENCES OF YOUTH RESTIVENESS

8.1 Background

In the prime years of restiveness in the Niger Delta (2000–2009), the Nigerian economy suffered an unprecedented fall in revenue earnings. Arising from restiveness in the region, oil production fell drastically as the activities of many oil-producing firms and multinational oil companies were restricted by the youths in the Niger Delta Region. Many of the oil-producing multinational oil companies reduced their production capacities as they were in many cases shut out from their activity zones, forcing them to reduce their sizes while cutting down on production.

The earlier well-intentioned advocacy by the Niger Delta youths for a better way of life for the region was hijacked by hooligans and criminals. This situation gave the government and all well-meaning citizens, as well as the international community, serious cause for concern. The situation assumed a criminal dimension as well as a crisis level with the spate of kidnappings and hostage takings for ransom, which reached a highly disturbing peak, sending danger signals to the international community.

The rise in global oil prices, occasioned by the Niger Delta youth restiveness, led to major distortions in the operations of major world economies. It also impacted the Niger Delta regional economy negatively with the withdrawal of expatriate workers in the energy and construction sectors of the region and shutting down of firms and retrenchment of workers. This condition culminated in the throwing out of more youths who were hitherto employed into the labour market, as well as the huge reduction in development funds paid to the Niger Delta states through the 13 percent derivation fund from the Federation Account.

It is important to note that Nigeria is a mono-product (crude oil) exporting country. The country's revenue earnings from oil, as earlier stated, average around 85 percent of total federal revenues earnings. Fluctuations in earnings from oil arising from fluctuations in oil production output due to activities of restive youths in the Niger Delta Region of Nigeria have caused tremendous fiscal apprehension in the country among the federal, state, and local governments. Since the country depends almost totally on oil revenue receipts, when it wants to share its revenue among the federating units (federal, state, and local governments), oil revenue earnings are seriously considered.

8.2 Nigeria's National Crime Record

The Nigerian national crime records of 2008 and 2009 show an outright upsurge in recorded crime nationally (Nigerian Police Force Annual Report, 2009). As in Tables 8.1 to 8.6, there are thirteen identified crime types in the country, which include: murder, manslaughter, attempted murder, suicide, attempted suicide, g/marm and wounding, assault, child stealing, slave dealing, rape and indecent assault, kidnapping, unilateral offences, and other offences. The crimes highlighted above were indicated per police command in the country. There are thirty-seven police command units in the country, indicating that each state and the federal capital territory has a command.

A global view of the tables shows that viewed from a state-by-state breakdown of crime, Akwa Ibom State in the South-South Region of the country had the highest number of murders (177) between 2008 and 2009. Anambra State came close in second place to Akwa Ibom on murder. Imo, Delta, and Lagos followed in that order. For kidnapping, another thriving crime in the country on which much of the discussion in this book is anchored, Rivers State came tops with 228 cases and Anambra State followed with 110 cases. Apart from Lagos, which followed with 57 cases, all the other South-South states were strongly indicated.

Further analyses of the data were considered to really identify and give weights to the regional spread and concentration of crime in and among the regions. Tables 8.2 and 8.3 show the regional data comparison. The South-South Zone, or the Niger Delta, ranks over and above other zones in murder with 501 murder cases. It is followed by the South Eastern Zone with 418 murder cases, then the North Eastern Zone with 353 murder cases. South-South Nigeria also led the statistics in attempted murder with 121 cases, followed by the South East with 82 cases, the South West with 47 cases, and the North East with 32 cases, while the North Central and North Western Zones recorded 8 and 3 cases respectively.

On kidnapping, the South-South region led the table with 346 cases from 2008–2009. Following the South-South Zone was the South Eastern Zone with 180 cases. The South Western Zone recorded 94 cases and the North Central Zone had 51 cases while North Eastern and North Western Zones had 37 and 5 cases respectively.

A breakdown of the crime record analyses shows that the South-South Zone ranked highest in notorious and notable crimes, especially murder, attempted murder, suicide, attempted suicide, assault, rape, kidnapping and even other offences. This text has taken time to discuss and set out the relationship between restiveness in the Niger Delta Region or South-South Nigeria and the crimes mentioned here. This statistics displayed here indicate that there is a positive relationship or correlation between restiveness and the various crimes highlighted in the crime record statistics. The indication is that if the right strategies are adopted to reduce restiveness in the regions, especially the South-South Zone, there will be serious reducing impact of the crimes recorded in the Zone.

Table 8.3 shows the distribution of crime by type, among the states of the South-South region. The intention here is to carefully analyze and determine which of the states in the region has more incidences of these crimes. The result here will give an indication into mitigating strategies that should be developed to curb and eradicate, where possible, crime in the states. In developing that synergy to combat crime in the region, it is very important and necessary to identify what crime is prone to which state and what strategies could be implemented in order to stop or inhibit crime migration from one state to another within the regional boundaries since it is easier for this to happen because of cultural and traditional linkages. This seamless cultural and traditional linkage helps to easily transfer lifestyle among and within the clans.

It is also interesting to note that crime might have some real and positive correlation with the economic status of the states. Akwa Ibom State recorded the highest number of murders in the Zone, specifically 177 cases. This is followed by Delta State with reported 148 cases, then Edo with 79 cases and Rivers with 51 cases.

On kidnapping, Rivers State recorded 228 cases in the period 2008-2009. Edo, Delta, and Akwa Ibom states followed with reported incidents of 44, 30, and 29 respectively. Notice that this report does not invalidate the serious and alarming kidnapping information reported in Akwa Ibom State for the year 2010. The later report is a follow-up to previous 2008-2009 data as reported by the police. The Akwa Ibom State-specific 2010 kidnapping report was necessitated by the growing concern to unravel the reason for the fast pace of growth of kidnapping in the state, which is regarded as strange in a state that have never been reported to be restive enough to attract the rate of crime (kidnapping and murder) experienced in 2010. Being the leading oil-producing state in the region and in Nigeria, it is necessary that we closely analyze the restiveness condition and conditions prevalent for such crime to thrive and grow in the state, if mitigating variables must be identified to either curb or totally eradicate the trend. It is also hoped that it will be an interesting study for other states that may eventually, like Akwa Ibom State, see themselves catapulting into the "rich bracket." It may also interest further studies to explain in quantitative terms if being rich (growth) has a positive correlation with crime and related activities.

Table 8.1: Police Crime Record–All States (2008-2009)

S/N	Command	Murder	Manslaughter	Att. Murder	Suicide	Att. Murder	G/ Marm, Wnding	Assault	Child Stealing	Slav Dealing	Rape & Indecent assault	Kidnapping	Untrl Offences	Other Offences
1	Abuja	52		1	12		155	202	2		22	20	19	107
2	A"ibom	177	1	62	8	21	100	320	18		93	29	234	10
3	Anambra	161		12	26		113	597	22		76	##	5	91
4	Adamawa	48	1	2	9	2	200	210			19	14	4	422
5	Abia	5		23			20	16	4		14	18		8
6	Bauchi	49	1	2	9	2	200	210			19	14	4	422
7	Benue	29			6		118	31			27	3	6	158
8	Borno	91			6	7	154	189			43	5	5	327
9	Bayelsa	37			6	2	44	583			43	5	5	327
10	C. River	9		9	25	2	83	2630	2		47	7	10	249
11	Delta	148	2	#	14	3	388	485	3		187	30	223	727
12	Edo	79		#	1		280	289			116	44		122
13	Enugu	35		#	1	1	87	401			45	14	10	47
14	Ebonyi	61		#	1		24	67			32	19	13	168
15	Ekiti	16		5	1	1	2	78	1		7	12		16
16	Gombe	42		#	6	19	7	311	1		29	19		15
17	Imo	156		6			179				29	19		15
18	Jigawa	50			9		104	102			62	2	6	11
19	Kaduna	75			5		80	56			48	4		33

S/N	Command	Murder	Mans-laughter	Att. Murder	Suicide	Att. Murder	G/ Marm, Wnding	Assault	Child Stealing	Slav Dealing	Rape & Indecent assault	Kidnapping	Untrl Offences	Other Offences
20	Kano	66			2		108	907			98		11	41
21	Katsina	32			9	1	64	61			27		8	25
22	Kebbi	17			1	2	49	79			6	2	14	52
23	Kogi	46		1			38	87	1		6	2	14	52
24	Kwara	2	4	2			787	631			16		22	60
25	Lagos	148	2	#	2	2	6373	###	11		566	57	405	561
26	Niger	53		1			116	12	2		51	15	2	56
27	Nasarawa	53		2			146	110	1		17	7	4	72
28	Ogun	53					189	158			44	12	7	1020
29	Ondo	26					43	69			22	10	11	108
30	Oyo	53		6	1		487	60			20	2	8	102
31	Osun	11		3			146	25			11	1	9	99
32	Plateau	32		2			87	91	1		10			87
33	Rivers	51				1	99	120	2		19	##	215	1001
34	Sokoto	33		3			107	115			50	1		38
35	Taraba	60	4		1		136	103			14	2	2	29
36	Yobe	63				1	151	103			14	2	2	29
37	Zamfara	36					35	51			10		3	87
	Total	38955												

Source: The Nigeria Police Force

137

Table 8.2: POLICE CRIME RECORD–ZONAL DISTRIBUTION (2008-2009)

S/N	Comnd	Murder	Mans-laughter	Att. Murder	Suicide	Att. Suicide	G/ Marm & Wnding	Assault	Child Stling	Slav. Dealing	Rape & Indt. assault	Kdnping. Offences	Unrl. Offences	Other Offences
1	South-South	501	3	121	59	29	994	4327	25		500	346	728	1,270
2	South-East	418		82	28	1	423	1614	27		196	180	28	329
3	South-West	307		47	4	4	7,240	4,888	11		670	94	440	1,906
4	North-Central	342	4	8	24	2	1,538	1,212	7		197	51	67	525
5	North-East	353	2	32	31	31	848	811	1		136	37	23	1,278
6	North West	353		3	21	3	467	1,315	1		253	5	42	254
	Total	234												

Table 8.3: POLICE CRIME RECORD–NIGER-DELTA (SOUTH-SOUTH STATES), 2008-2009

S/N	Command	Murder	Mansl	Att. Murder	Suicide	Att. Suicide	G/Marm & Wnding	Assault	Child Stealing	Slav Dealing	Rape & Ind. assault	Kidn	Unna. Offences	Other Offences
1	A'Ibom	177	1	62	8	21	100	320	18		93	29	234	10
2	Bayelsa	37			6	2	44	189			38	8	46	161
3	C" River	9		9	6	2	83	583	2		47	7	10	249
4	Delta	148	2	36	25	3	388	2630	3		187	30	223	727
5	Edo	79		14	14		280	485			116	44	223	122
6	Rivers	51				1	99	120	2		19	228	215	1001
	Total	501	3	121	59	29	994	4327	25		500	346	728	1270

FIGURE 8.1: DISTRIBUTION OF KIDNAPPING AND MURDER CASES BY GEOPOLITICAL ZONES IN NIGERIA (2008-2009)

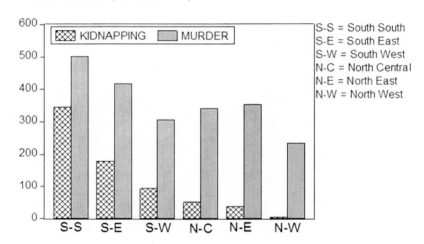

FIGURE 8.2: DISTRIBUTION OF KIDNAPPING AND MURDER CASES IN CORE NIGER DELTA (SOUTH-SOUTH) STATES, 2008-2009

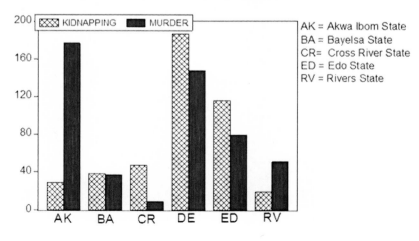

Table 8.4: POLICE CRIME RECORD–SOUTH EAST STATES (2008-2009)

S/N	Command	murder	Man-slaughter	Alt. murder	suicide	Alt suic	G/Marm/Wding	Assault	Child Sting	Slave dealing	Rape & Indecent Assauit	Knping	Unrl offences	Other offences
1	Anambra	16		12	26		113	597	22		76	110	5	91
2	Abia	5		23			20	16	4		14	18		8
3	Enugu	35		21	1		87	289			45	14	10	47
4	Ebonyi	61		20	1		24	401			32	19	13	168
5	Imo	156		6			179	311	1		29	19		15
	Total	418		82	28		423	1614	27		196	180	28	329

Table 8.5: POLICE CRIME RECORD–SOUTH WEST STATES (2008-2009).

S/N	Command	murder	Man-slaughter	Alt. murder	suicide	Alt suicide	G/Marm/ Wnding	Assault	Child Stealing	Slave dealing	Rape & Indecent Assault
1	Ekiti	16	2	5	1	1	2	67			7
2	Lagos	148		33	2	2	6.373	4511	11		566
3	Ogun	53					189	156			44
4	Ondo	26		6	1	1	43	69			22
5	Oyo	536		3	1		487	60			20
6	Osun	11		3	4		146	25			11
	Total	307	2	47		4	7.24				

Table 8.6: POLICE CRIME RECORD–NORTH CENTRAL STATES (2008-2009)

S/N	Comnd.	murder	Man-slaughter	Alt. murder	suicide	Alt suicide	G/Marm/ Wnding	Assault	Child Stling.	Slave dealings	Rape & Indct. Assauit	Kidnaping	Unturl offences	Other offences
1	Abuja	52		1	12		156	202		2	22	20	19	107
2	Kogi	46		1			38	87			6	2	14	52
3	Benue	29			6		116	31			27	3	6	158
4	Plateau	32		2			87	91	1		10			87
5	Niger	536		1			116	12	2		51	15	2	56
6	Nassarawa	53		2			146	2110	1		17	7	4	72
7	Kaduna	75	4			5	80	56			48	4		33
8	Kwara	2		2			787	631			16		22	60

143

Table 8.7: POLICE CRIME RECORD—NORTH EAST STATES (2008-2009)

S/N	Command	murder	Man-slaughter	Alt. murder	suicide	Alt suicide	G/Marm/ Wnding	Assault	Child Stealing	Slave dealing	Rape & Indecent Assault	Kidnaping	Unnatural offences	Other offences
1	Borno	91			5	7	154	107			43	5	5	327
2	Bauchi	49	1	2	9	2	200	210			19	14	4	422
3	Adamawa	48		2	9	2	210	210			19	14	4	422
4	Tarba	60		4	1		136	103			14	2	2	29
5	Gombe	42		24	6	19	7	78	1		23	2	4	37
6	Yobe	63	1			1	151	103			18		4	41
	Total		2											

Table 8.8: POLICE CRIME RECORD–NORTH WESTERN STATES (2008-2009)

S/N	Command	murder	Man-slaughter	Alt. murder	suicide	Alt. suicide	G/Marm/ Wunding	Assault	Child Stealing	Slave dealing	Rape & Indecent Assauit	Kidnaping	Unnatural offences	O ofnces
1	Sokoto	33		3			107	115			50	1		38
2	Kebi	17			1	2	49	79	1		6	2	14	52
3	Zamfara	36					35	51			10		3	87
4	Kassina	32			9	1	64	61			27		8	26
5	Jigawa	30			9		104	102			62	2	6	11
6	Kano	66			2		108				89		11	41
	Total							907						

8.2.1 "Crowding Out" of Businesses in the Niger Delta

As explained earlier in the text, restiveness in Nigeria was indicated by violence, kidnapping, piracy, armed robbery, communal wars, illegal oil bunkering and other acts of lawlessness. These activities turned the Niger Delta into a somewhat war territory and a place of hopelessness where the inhabitants knew no peace with unfortunate circumstances bothering on insecurity. This uncertainty created enormous anxiety in the psyche of the inhabitants of the region, mostly businesses, whose main aim of staying in the region is to make profit. Aside from the fact that firms operating in the region started scaling down on their installed capacities utilization due to increased cost of doing business occasioned by youth restiveness, a substantial number of the aggregate demand force started waning, as people with effective demand started exiting the region in order not to be caught in the ensuing struggle and crossfire between government forces and the restive youths. With decreased aggregate demand and increased cost of doing business, business turnover in the region was no longer desirable or profitably encouraging. This caused businesses to start relocating from the region, indicating the "crowding out."

The effects of the crowding out of businesses from the Niger Delta Region impacted seriously on the economy in the following ways:

1. Increased unemployment occasioned by the huge layoff of workers by firms emigrating from the Niger Delta—for instance, when Julius Berger pulled out from all their contract sites in Rivers, Bayelsa and Delta states.

2. Abandonment of projects of both government and oil multinational oil companies by contractors and sub-contractors.

3. Decreased tax earnings to governments of the region as most multinational businesses that would have attracted tax to the South-South regional governments were relocated to be anchored or done in another region in the country. For example, the signing of contracts by the multinational companies that would have attracted good taxes to the states hosting those companies were diverted to other states in other regions where security and safety was guaranteed.

4. Decreased earnings to the state governments in the region due to the decrease in oil production, making the state governments unable to render promised expected services to the people of the region.

5. Encouragement of and intense cultivation of the underground economy (black market) in all facets of the economic life of the region due to scarcity of all lawful means to good livelihood, since lawlessness had taken over the region, making it difficult even to implement the country's constitution. It created a situation where governments had to be negotiating and working with criminal elements of the restiveness to secure favour or LTOs and keep power from the criminals. Once some governments got those endorsements, they became wild and also unlawful, dealing with political opponents as if they were dealing with criminals with no respect for the rule of law.

8.2.2 Emergence of Armed Militia and Criminal Elements in Nigeria

Youth restiveness in the Niger Delta was initially seen as a genuine struggle by a people for basic rights in a multi-ethnic society wherein the Niger Delta Region constitute the minority group. As criminality crept into the struggle, the demand for arms and ammunitions became an issue to use in prosecuting looting and protecting the loots from others.

Aside from inter-cult, intra-cult, inter-criminal, and intra-criminal group struggles, the action permeated into and through the region, culminating in inter- and intra-community wars and struggles and even armed conflicts between most criminal-minded youths and the military who were posted by the federal government to the region to quell restiveness and maintain peace.

A clear indication of the preponderance of arms in the region was demonstrated during the amnesty program of the Federal Republic of Nigeria under President Umaru Musa Yar'dua for Niger Delta militants in 2009. This program was intended at convincing the restive youths of the Niger Delta Region to lay down their arms and embrace peace. The amount of arms recovered from the exercise was massive and significant. Even the military expressed shock and surprise at the amount and sophistication of arms that were recovered from the repentant militants.

8.2.3 Proliferation of Arms in the Niger Delta

The ensuing period of deep restiveness in the Niger Delta Region witnessed intensified acquisition and proliferation of small and medium arms in the region. Though the source of arms infiltration remain illegal, the arms were significant.

An initial indication of the significance of the arms build-up was the conscious and intensified arms struggle between the restive youths (including militants, illegal oil bunkerers, sea pirates, armed robbers, and local community militia groups) and government security agencies in the region. Between 2006 and 2008, the arms conflict became more intense with large quantities of arms and ammunitions used and expended by both sides (government and the restive youths) with the government military yet unable to subdue the strength of the restive youths.

With the worsening and persisting trend of fortified and well-armed youths, the federal government in 2009 decided to and implemented the ingenious strategy of substituting peace for war. This government (President Umaru Musa Yar'dua's) quite different from earlier ones in the country decided to adopt the Amnesty Program for the militant Niger Delta youths. The Amnesty program that was tossed as a recipe for peace in the Niger Delta was characterized by the surrender of arms for cash and development. This program unexpectedly survived and succeeded exceedingly as tones of light and medium weapons were recovered from the youths in the Niger Delta Region. Even when it is argued by many antagonists of the Amnesty program that the program did not lead to the full or optimum recovery of even a quarter of arms held by the militant youths of the Niger Delta, it could be generally argued that the quantity of arms and ammunition surrendered by the youths was significant and frightening, and an indication that something positive has started which successive governments should build on. Also, the unprecedented vouches of surrender by ex-militant warlords and leaders were enough encouragement to strengthen successive government to sustain this program and also fine-tune it where necessary to get desired results.

8.2.4 Reduction of Oil Production Capacity

From 2006, oil production index of the Federal Republic of Nigeria dipped seriously and steeply. Increased restiveness and tension in the region ensued decline in oil production as many oil-producing companies vacated the Niger Delta due to restiveness, shutting-in production in some cases and reducing installed capacity production in the other.

In addition to the reduction in production capacity of the multinational oil companies, the youths also undertook targeted vandalism of oil installations, blow-up of oil pipelines and outright blockage or stoppage of oil companies from producing as well as servicing firms from working on oil platforms, installations, and infrastructure requiring urgent attention.

Table 8.9 shows the loss that accrued to revenue earnings of the federal government of Nigeria due to restiveness activities of youths in the Niger Delta Region. From 2006, the region experienced a peak in the activities of restiveness including: kidnapping, armed robbery, oil theft, illegal bunkering and all sort of criminality aimed at disorientating government and the oil companies, with the aim of forcing them to flee from the region, while leaving its rich installed oil resources open to be raped by the violent youths.

The Technical Committee on the Niger Delta set up by the President Yar'dua administration put the estimated loss of seven hundred thousand barrels of oil per day in the region for 2006. This culminated to a total loss of $17,120,320,000 revenue in 2006 that would have accrued to the federation account. This loss is more than what is required by the federal government to generate ten thousand megawatts of electricity in the country—enough to ensure uninterrupted power supply in the country with its attendant positive multiplier effects on the economy.

The total of this oil revenue loss included that lost to shut-in production and that lost to illegal oil bunkering. Table 8.10 shows that in 2006, 25,900,000 barrels of oil were lost to bunkering. This amounted to $1,978,191,600.

In 2007, a total of 255,500,000 barrels of oil were lost to youth restiveness. Total amount lost was $18,805,262,000 billion (Table 8.11). This indicates about a 10 percent increase in losses accruing to the revenue of the federal government of Nigeria. This amount, if earned, would have helped tremendously in resolving the infrastructure challenges of the federal government as well as helped finance the begging issues of development of the Niger Delta Region.

It is remarkable to note that from March 2007, the price of Nigeria Crude started appreciating, climaxing at $88.84 in November 2007 (Table 8.11). This was well above the benchmark of $55 per barrel adopted for the federal government budget. Instead of the country gaining from the oil market price appreciation, caused by stochastic factors that were not accounted for in earlier price forecast of the market, it lost to youth restiveness (indicated by shut-ins and illegal bunkering).

The loss in revenue earnings from oil continued in 2008 (Table 8.12). The dollar value for the loss stood at $20,720,842,000 in 2008 (Table 8.13), which was a progression from the 2006 and 2007 values. In 2008, the international oil market price experienced tremendous leap or appreciation in the price level. If Nigeria had produced oil at its optimum level or at the OPEC-approved production quota, it would have experienced tremendous boom in earnings from the resource. In that year (2008), oil prices averaged at $100 per barrel. Nigeria, however, could not derive commensurate benefits from this price regime, as it could not produce enough even to meet its OPEC-approved quota due to youth restiveness in the Niger Delta Region.

Table 8.12 presents a more explicit picture of loses experienced in the Nigerian oil sector. From a monthly optimum production capacity of 1,168,535,820 bbls, only 768,741,187 bbls was produced. This left the country's oil sector with a whooping shut-in of 399,794,633 bbls for the year 2008.

From Table 8.14, it can be noted that in only two months, January and February of 2009, a whopping 71,482,363 bbls oil were lost to shut-ins, arising from youth restiveness as alerted by the oil companies that they said was occasioned by oil pipeline vandalism, operational constraints, and the Niger Delta crises, as shown and highlighted by the Technical Committee on the Niger Delta that was set up in 2009 by the federal government.

This glaring and expository data, therefore, informed the government to devise sustainable methodologies to stop or reduce youth restiveness in the Niger Delta Region to the barest minimum so she could produce oil at its optimum level. Recall that oil is the major revenue-earning sector for the government of Nigeria.

8.2.5 Militarization of the Niger Delta Region

The arms situation and the ensuing arms conflict between the Niger Delta youths and the Nigerian military have caused serious concerns. Inhabitants of the Niger Delta Region do not feel safe any longer except with guns or other protective gadgets. This prevailing condition has tended, over the years of restiveness, to encourage youths and even children into the psychology of arms and conflict.

Table 8.9: Quantity of Oil Loss in Barrels Per Day/Amount in US Dollars for 2006

Months	Estimate Qty of barrels of Oil loss Per Day	Total Barrels of Oil Loss for the Month	OPEC basket Price for Bonny Light crude oil for the Month in US$	Total Amount for the month in US $
January	700,000	21,700,000	64.04	1,389,668,000
February	700,000	20,300,000	62.12	1,261,036,000
March	700,000	21,700,000	63.80	1,384,460,000
April	700,000	21,700,000	71.80	1,507,800,000
May	700,000	21,700,000	71.75	1,556,975,000
June	700,000	21,700,000	70.22	1,474,620,000
July	700,000	21,700,000	75.49	1,638,133,000
August	700,000	21,700,000	75.29	1,633,793,000
September	700,000	21,700,000	63.87	1,341,270,000
October	700,000	21,700,000	58.57	1,270,969,000
November	700,000	21,700,000	60.32	1,266,720,000
December	700,000	21,700,000	64.28	1,394,876,000
Grand Total				$17,120,320,000

Source: Report of Technical Committee on the Niger Delta

Table 8.10: Quantity of Oil Loss in Barrels Per Day/Amount in US Dollars for 2006

Months	Estimate Qty of barrels of Oil loss Per Day	Total Barrels of Oil Loss for the Month	OPEC basket Price for Bonny Light crude oil for the Month in US$	Total Amount for the month in US $
January	700,000	2,170,000	64.04	138,966,800
February	700,000	2,170,000	62.12	126,103,600
March	700,000	2,170,000	63.8	138,446,000
April	700,000	2,170,000	71.8	150,780,000
May	700,000	2,170,000		155,697,500
June	700,000	2,170,000	70.22	147,462,000
July	700,000	2,170,000	75.49	163,813,300
August	700,000	2,170,000	75.29	163,379,300
September	700,000	2,170,000	63.87	134,127,000
October	700,000	2,170,000	58.57	126,096,900
November	700,000	2,170,000	60.32	126,672,000
December	700,000	2,170,000	64.28	139,487,600
Grand Total				$1,978,191,600

Source: Report of Technical Committee on the Niger Delta

Table 8.11 Quantity of Oil Loss in Barrels Per Day/Amount in US Dollars for 2007

Months	Estimate Qty of barrels of Oil loss Per Day	Total Barrels of Oil Loss for the Month	OPEC basket Price for Bonny Light crude oil for the Month in US$	Total Amount for the mnoth in US $
January	700,000	21,700,000	56.18	1,219,106,000
February	700,000	19,600,000	59.58	1,167,768,000
March	700,000	21,700,000	64.59	1,401,603,000
April	700,000	21,700,000	70.01	1,470,210,000
May	700,000	21,700,000	70.03	1,519,651,000
June	700,000	21,700,000	74.45	1,583,450,000
July	700,000	21,700,000	79.21	1,718,857,000
August	700,000	21,700,000	73.34	1,591,478,000
September	700,000	21,700,000	79.87	1,677,270,000
October	700,000	21,700,000	79.32	1,721,244,000
November	700,000	21,700,000	88.84	1,865,640,000
December	700,000	21,700,000	87.05	1,888,985,000
Grand Total		255,500,000		$18,805,262,000

Source: Report of Technical Committee on the Niger Delta

Table 8.12 NNPC's Monthly Production Profile vs Shut-in for Year 2008

Months	Monthly production	Overall daily production capacity (bbls)	Monthly production capacity (bbls)	Shut-in (bbls)
January	67,122,292	3,201,468	99,245,508	32,123,216
February	60,380,977	3,201,468	92,842,572	32,461,595
March	64,000,319	3,201,468	99,245,508	35,245,189
April	58,930,055	3,201,468	96,044,040	37,113,985
May	63,636,321	3,201,468	96,044,040	32,407,719
June	60,542,039	3,201,468	96,044,040	35,502,001
July	65,961,347	3,201,468	99,245,508	33,284,161
August	65,241,907	3,201,468	99,245,508	34,003,601
September	65,157,212	3,201,468	96,044,040	30,886,828
October	70,192,271	3,201,468	99,245,508	29,053,237
November	64,257,050	3,201,468	96,044,040	31,786,990
December	63,319,397	3,201,468	99,245,508	35,926,111
Total	796,741,187	38,417,616	1,168,535,820	399,794,633

Source: Report of the Technical Committee on the Niger Delta

Table 8.13 Quantity of Oil Loss in Barrels Per Day/Amount in US Dollars for 2008

Months	Estimate Qty of barrels of Oil loss Per Day	Total Barrels of Oil Loss for the Month	OPEC basket Price for Bonny Light crude oil for the Month in US$	Total Amount for the month in US $
January	700,000	21,700,000	88.35	1,917,195,000
February	700,000	20,700,000	90.64	1,839,992,000
March	700,000	21,700,000	99.03	2,148,951,000
April	700,000	21,700,000	105.16	2,208,630,000
May	700,000	21,700,000	119.39	2,590,763,000
June	700,000	21,700,000	128.33	2,694,930,000
July	700,000	21,700,000	131.22	2,847,474,000
August	700,000	21,700,000	112.41	1,633,793,000
September	700,000	21,700,000	96.85	2,439,297,000
Grand Total				$20,720,842,000

Source: Report of Technical Committee on the Niger Delta

Tables 8.14 NNPC's Monthly Production Profile vs Shut-in for January/February 2009

Months	Monthly production	Overall daily production capacity (bbls)	Monthly production capacity (bbls)	Shut-in (bbls)
January	63,042,650	3,201,468	99,245,508	36,202,858
February	57,563,067	3,201,469	92,842,572	35,279505
Total	120,605,717	6,402,936	192,088,080	71,482,363

Source: Report of the Technical Committee on the Niger Delta
Note: Shut-in due to

1. *Pipeline Vandalism*
2. *Operational Constraint*
3. *Niger Delta Crises*

The Niger Delta Region, before the federal government of Nigeria's amnesty program of 2009, had assumed the status of a war territory as the region was completely militarized. This had brought about the ravaging of the social fabric of the region, causing undue and unnecessary tension while raising more serious conflict tendencies.

8.2.6 Relocation of Oil Companies and Other Multinationals from the Niger Delta

One of the key byproducts of the restiveness in the Niger Delta Region has been the crowding out or emigration of Oil Multinationals from the region. Where companies neither operate profitably and sustainably, nor able to take full responsibility for the livelihood or well-being of her workers, they are bound to seek an alternative operational environment that will provide them the ambience to engage in profitable and sustainable business while being assured of security of life and property in their business.

With increased restive activities like kidnapping, piracy, communal clashes, violence, etc., in the Niger Delta Region, many firms relocated their operations away from the region. Many were oil-producing and oil-servicing companies. Also affected were those companies whose existence depended on the economies of scale of the large multinational oil companies and others. It is remarkable to note that many of the companies relocated their important working and administrative bases away from the Niger Delta Region, pitching their emergency activities in places like Lagos and Abuja (the federal capital territory).

This action, apart from countering the clamour of the Niger Delta people to coerce the oil multinational oil companies to move their operational headquarters to the Niger Delta Region, also resulted in massive destruction of the ailing economies of the Niger Delta states. Such relocation led to the following:

(i) Increase in unemployment
(ii) Reduction in tax earnings of the states of the Niger Delta
(iii) Fall in business activities and shrinking of the private sector
(iv) Abandonment of projects, including community development projects anchored by oil multinational oil companies and government

8.2.7 Increased Cost Component in the Operating Businesses" Profit Equation in the Niger Delta Region

The youth restiveness in the Niger Delta Region had serious negative impact on the cost of doing business in the region. To secure an LTO, most firms had to pay more in order to be able to operate. They had to spend more on security, to secure their facilities and lives of their personnel as well as pay more hazard allowances and bonuses to workers who were ready to dare the restive conditions in the region. With decreasing earnings from oil, occasioned by falling prices, and the inability to produce at installed capacity (or, in that case, the OPEC-approved production quota for the country), the profit function shrank seriously. As revenue decreased, cost of doing business in the Niger Delta increased, occasioned by issues already discussed above. This condition led to a fall in the profit made by these firms - indicating serious lull in business activities. From an economic theory paradigm, this reduction in business activities by the core businesses that hold the economy of the region will eventually lead to reduction of aggregate demand, resulting in fall in effective demand, inventory accumulation, general business failure, and general fall in living standards of the people. This condition had been very obvious in the Niger Delta Region during the days of restiveness.

All these put together are having serious consequences on the economy of Nigeria. For instance, frequent pipeline vandalisms have resulted in the shutting down of some of Nigeria's oil refinery plants; as well as the reduction of electricity generated by plants, which depend on gas. The toll on the nation has been enormous.

This, coupled with the flight of expatriates has also affected the supply of Nigeria's crude in the international market, thus cutting down on revenue generations.

In a BBC report of 21st May 2007, it was said that international oil price rose above $70 as tension escalated in the Niger Delta. The sharp price increase followed the kidnapping by Gunmen of two Indian employees of the Eleme Petrochemical in Port Harcourt.

On the cost of the Niger Delta insurgency to the Nigerian Economy, the Central Bank of Nigeria (CBN) has said that revenue accruing from sale of the nations" crude oil reduced by 20.5 percent from Nl.280 trillion to N1.018 trillion at the end of first quarters of 2007, when compared to the level in the preceding quarter. (Thisday Newspaper, 9th July 2007).

Quoting the apex Bank, the paper said the drop was caused by the protracted crisis in the Niger Delta Region. It further stated that the reduction in oil earnings affected the total federally-collected revenue, which stood at Nl.225

trillion by the end of the period under review. Oil revenue accounted for 83.2 percent of this figure.

Giving an elaborate picture of the situation, in its Economic report for the first Quarter of 2007, the apex bank attributed the fall in oil receipts to the cut in the volume of oil production resulting from the continued restiveness in the Niger Delta Region.

So far, over 200 foreigners, mostly oil workers had been seized by militants in the last two years and more than 1,000 had fled the country (Vanguard Newspaper, 17th July 2007).

In the same 17th July 2007 edition of the Vanguard Newspapers, it was reported that beside the trillions of naira that have been lost by the country due to the crisis, the Niger Delta states have been suffering as a result of the emergency. The implication is that since all the states in region have been failing in their oil production quota, their 13 percent derivation fund will also be reduced, and the fast pace of social and economic development, which was the hallmark of the democratic political era, will be slowed down.

Working in an unsafe environment will also place the oil companies in a continuous unwarranted tension and anxiety that renders the operations uncoordinated and stressful. As a result, the economy suffers and the people in the lower social cadre whose main means of survival are tied to menial jobs associated with the oil industry are rendered redundant.

Also affected are various developmental projects in the region. The security situation in the Niger Delta is taking a huge toll on the economy as nine key projects, worth over N266bn, are currently stalled because contractors handling them cannot stay on site (Madunagu, 2007). Some of the projects include the dualization of the East-West road, the rehabilitation of the Port Harcourt International Airport, construction of Eleme Junction flyover, dualization of Onne Port access road, completion of outstanding works on the dualization of the Benin-Warri Road, and the construction of the Bodo-Bonny Road.

Chapter 9

SUGGESTED WAYS OUT

9.1 Background

Given the careful analytical study in this text that has thrown up issues for common knowledge and comprehension, this chapter brings up the very core and cogent suggestions through which restiveness, especially that of the Niger Delta Region, could be significantly contained. Most of the suggested panaceas to the problem and issue of restiveness are derived from our earlier analyses and studies in this text. Also, some suggestions are derived and inspired from other literature on the Niger Delta.

In the earlier chapters, we tried to show the merits and demerits of youth restiveness. Although this text acknowledges some positive economic benefits of restiveness, the negative effects of this phenomenon, both economic and social, on a macroeconomic scale, far outweighs any positive benefits that would have accrued there-from. This calls for the need to suggest strategies that will help in abating and eradicating restiveness in the Niger Delta and the possibility of its replication anywhere in Nigeria.

Although we have been able to discover and underscore some level of benefits to households and communities arising from restiveness, it is mostly in a microeconomic sense. The benefit so recorded is not enough to affect the macro-economy of the Nigerian Federation when aggregated. Thus, it could be discovered, as in Chapter 8, how several micro institutions have collapsed in the country as a result of the negative effect of youth restiveness in the Niger Delta Region. Recall that Nigeria depends on the revenue accruing to her petroleum products sales. Oil revenue constitutes over 85 percent of Nigerian government earnings and thus becomes a very strategic product that any distortion in its market can cause serious shock on the Nigerian economy. We have also seen in Chapter 8 how youth restiveness in the Niger Delta has led to serious reduction in oil production levels, with the implication of reduced revenue earnings from the non-renewal product. The impact of this reduced revenue accruing to the federation account is multivariate. This reality highlights, therefore, the obvious importance of the oil sector to the Nigerian economy and why all must be done to stabilize the sector in order to be able to provide the tools for the country's economic development. Since youth restiveness has been clearly indicated as the main cause of the oil sector plunge in Nigeria, a situation confirmed by the Nigerian government while granting amnesty to the Niger Delta militants in 2009, it therefore behooves this text, if it intends to conclude appropriately, to suggest sustainable ways out of the youth restiveness in the Niger Delta Region, which, apart from the amnesty granted, will thoroughly and permanently disengage the Niger Delta youths from youth restiveness while engaging them in sustainable and legal economic ventures.

9.2 Suggested Ways Out of Youth Restiveness in the Niger Delta

In this section of the chapter, incisive analyses deriving from the findings in the earlier chapters of this text and other literature on the subject matter will be adopted and adapted to identify possible solutions to—"ways out" of—the present youth restiveness problems and situation in the Niger-Delta region of Nigeria. This text has taken into account all variables that constituted restiveness function in the Niger Delta Region (kidnapping, robbery, violence, disruption of oil prospecting and producing activities, etc.), and the causative factors that engender the deepening of those variables. It is the identification of the problems that have helped in modeling appropriate solution and strategies in solving these problems as outlined in this chapter.

9.2.1 Reform of Legislation Governing Petroleum Activities in Nigeria

Existing legislation in the oil sector has been obviously repressive to the various sectors and stakeholders in the oil community business in the country. Such legislations had given room for non-participation of communities in the activities taking place in their lands and the continuous emission and flaring of the nation's gas resources—as it is cheaper to flare than gather for production—that contributes to the abuse of the environment, especially that of the oil-producing and adjoining communities. It has visited untold hardship on these oil-producing communities and adjoining neighbourhoods. In many cases communities are trapped between the oil companies and their government for who should provide what (especially social and public goods) to the communities.

The non-participation of communities in the oil sector activities, as is made possible by existing and enabling current legislation on petroleum activities in Nigeria, had opened up the multinational oil companies that operate in the communities to attacks by restive community youths and militants who by their activities almost totally crippled the activities of these companies as well as the earnings of the federal government from oil sales—oil being the only foreign revenue earner for the country.

It is, however, heartwarming to note that in 2009, the federal government of Nigeria, under the regime of President Umaru Musa Yar'dua, proposed the Petroleum Industry Bill (PIB) to the National Assembly for passage into law. The bill was to garnish the amnesty program of the federal government for the militant youths of the Niger Delta Region in order to assuage the overwhelming youth restiveness in the Niger Delta, as it affected oil production and, specifically, foreign revenue earnings. The highpoint of the PIB is the intention to allow the communities fully participate in the activities of oil industries operating in their domains, while sharing in the earnings from oil from the federal government in the form of royalty of 10 percent. If this bill is passed into law and conscientiously implemented, it is strongly hoped that it will reduce the restiveness to a very significant level.

9.2.2 Review of the Resource Distribution Model of the Region

The resource distribution model of the region, as earlier discussed in this text, shows that the greater percentage of the region's population, which includes youths and women, do not have any significant share in the benefits accruing in the region from the resources derived there from. As presently constituted, the oil sector has no room for the participation of these vulnerable groups (women and youths). They are either considered as not competitively educated enough to get employed in the oil companies operating in their areas, or not competent enough to engage in contracts and sub-contracts in the sector. Also, they are seen as not connected enough to break through into government and politics as well as not being experienced enough to secure employment in government establishments and even the organized private sector employments. The deceit that comes out so easily in this posturing is that once the youths become restive and strike to demand for some rights, several uncoordinated concessions are made by both the multinational oil corporations and government to accommodate the restive youths. In these cases, they create "aspirin solutions" that create more problems than solutions in the communities and regions. Also, the responsible youth and female populations in the communities are left unattended, because they are not hostile, creating, therefore, serious and damaging jealousies, resentment, and envy, compounding the strife among and within the communities and regions.

It is therefore important and pertinent that a comprehensive reward and accommodating structure be developed as is being proposed in the PIB, to take into account the optimum sharing of benefits accruing from the region's oil proceeds to ensure equity and common participation by every strata in these region. The Nigerian government should ensure that the stakeholders in the communities are made to secure common participation in the production and distribution of the wealth of the region. This will secure the desired sustainable LTO as well as community ownership of the resources embedded in the community. The communities that are mostly populated by the youths and women will, therefore, see the oil installations of the multinational oil companies and government as part of their own, as they see themselves as part owners of the projects as well as earning their living from their operations.

9.2.3 The Reward System

It is pathetic to note that the reward system in Nigeria and very importantly the Niger Delta Region is a complete departure from international best practices. In many of the Nigeria and Niger Delta cases, people are rewarded for violence. It is only when there is restiveness (violence, kidnapping, riots, etc.) that the government and oil multinational oil companies in the region react and move to reward the restive stock in order to restore peace and earn LTOs. It has been observed that in all cases in the Niger Delta Region, the peace bought is unsustainable. For instance, in cases of oil spill, there are varied controversies that tend to create multiple problems where oil companies ignore oil spills, even when such destroy the environment and ecosystem and tend to dislocate the employment sources of the locals. Cases abound in the Niger Delta Region, where these multinational oil companies, apart from ignoring such spills, abandon the communities and arrogantly refuse to compensate for harm and destruction done to the environment, life, and properties. This scenario breeds contemptuous acrimony between the communities' restive youths and the multinational oil companies and government, when these communities know fully well that international best practices for oil operations require that oil corporations, apart from remediation of the environment that their activities have destroyed, should also pay compensation to owners of resources that such activities destroyed. A recent case of BP oil spill in the Gulf of Mexico in 2009, where the American government ordered BP to pay compensation to owners of destroyed properties while remediating the environment, is a standard case to note and the anchor of argument in the Niger Delta Region, whose communities have continually lost in the quest for fair practices when involved in environmental dislocation by the oil corporations. This clearly indicates apparent disparity in laws governing global oil operations (the international best practices laws) and the Nigerian oil business laws.

A clear case in point is the 2010 oil spill by Exxon-Mobil Oil Corporation that particularly affected the communities, marine life, sources of livelihood, and the environment along the Atlantic Coast off the Gulf of Guinea, including communities in Ibeno Local Government Area of Akwa Ibom State. The very damaging effects of this oil spill have been arrogantly ignored by Exxon-Mobil. Currently, they are usurping government might to ignore the affected communities and people. Rather than adopt best practices to solve this problem as is done internationally, they have in most cases decided to bribe the communities with town hall building, sharing the contracts among themselves, government agents, and influential community leaders, with total non-commitment to environmental issues and people's means of livelihood destroyed by the spill.

There is need for a structural change in the country's reward system, especially as it concerns the majority of the population in the Niger Delta Region (youths and women). Rewards should not only be for violence. The government and the oil multinational oil companies should consider, very importantly, rewarding peace. For instance, in the amnesty program of the federal government of Nigeria for the Niger Delta militant youths, only violent youths are considered. There is no consideration for the non-militant but equally aggrieved youths, who refused to join in violence and atrocious agitations in the region. If they are left unattended to, this group will constitute the future problem of the region. Also, the reward system should not only target politicians, chiefs, and businessmen the region, since all or most of their earnings (as indicated in our study) are not domiciled in the region. The women and youths who live and operate in these communities should be encouraged, as this will enhance grow and improve the local economy for quick economic recovery.

9.2.4 Boundary Demarcation

There is need for proper boundary demarcation, delineation, and adjustments to avoid the recurring cases of boundary and allied conflicts. There are serious contentious conflicts in the Niger Delta Region arising from boundary agitations. It should be noted that several years after creating the oil-bearing states of the Niger Delta, no distinct and defined boundaries have been drawn. Cases abound where nearly all the component states of the Niger Delta Region are in conflict. The conflict arises mostly from arguments or contentions on ownership of oil wells and oil and gas related resources. For instance, there is boundary conflict between Delta and Bayelsa states arising from oil resource ownership dispute. There is conflict between Rivers and Bayelsa states on similar oil properties ownership. There is also the conflict between Akwa Ibom State and Rivers State on the one hand as well as Akwa Ibom and Cross River states on the other hand arising from similar oil property ownership. The major reason, therefore, for these boundary conflicts remains the struggle for oil and oil-related property resource.

Aside from inter-states disputes, there are mounting intra-state disputes among the various oil-bearing communities: inter- and intra-communal conflicts and wars arising from boundary agitations. Wherever oil and gas related properties are located in the Niger Delta Region, boundary related conflicts have been a common phenomenon. Conflicts around the Kula, Bille and other surrounding communities on oil resource ownership in Rivers State, as well as that of Odioma, Obioku, and Nembe communities in Bayelsa State, and Esit Eket, Eket, Mbo, and Ibeno communities in Akwa Ibom State, are classical cases where agitations and conflicts are growing rapidly and wildly as a result of the failure or inability of the appropriate government institution(s) to determine communities and states boundaries, especially where oil property resources are found and located. Such crises develop into damaging proportions where communities even sponsor and arm youths to fight for their perceived rights. After the fight, the same weapons, which were not retrieved, are used by the youths to commit crime.

9.2.5 Identify and Reprimand Sponsors of Youth Restiveness in the Niger Delta

It has been positively and variedly identified that unscrupulous and self-seeking politicians and community leaders are in the fore of youth restiveness in the Niger Delta Region. It has also been strongly alleged and commented in literature that they instigate the youths to see restiveness as the sole solution to all their problems. In many cases, the picture is painted to make the youths believe that whatever negative action they will take will be for their good and that of their communities. This encourages the youths who follow their sponsors blindly. Once these sponsors, who are usually politicians (as variously indicated by commentators on youth restiveness in the Niger Delta), succeed in enticing these youths, they start using them for their personal gains and agenda. Politicians have been positively identified as those who have contributed immensely to youth restiveness in the Niger Delta. They are said to and known to use the youths as thugs to commit electoral violence, thereby distorting free and fair elections. Besides, they use the youths to engage in communal and tribal wars, whenever they think or find out that they have lost out, even genuinely, in the struggle to control the oil-benefits economics of the region. Cases abound where political and community leaders clash over ownership of oil property resources that bear cash proceeds to the owners of such landed properties. In order to take control of the situation and divert such gains to themselves, even wrongly, these politicians and community leaders engage the youths to fight—acquiring for them, in the process, light, medium and heavy combat weapons to prosecute their assignments. It is remarkable to note that in many cases, once the battle is over, the sponsors, who only know the rule of engagement and absolutely lack of knowledge of the rule of disengagement, become unable to retrieve the weapons they bought for the youths, and also become unable to debrief these youths out of restive engagement. This condition is indicated in the wild increase in cases of cultism, gangsterism, and militancy that have emerged in recent years from the activities of youth restiveness in the region. These new extracts of restiveness (cultism, gangsterism, and militancy) are assuming fatal and damaging dimensions. Cultism has claimed more lives than clashes between the restive youths and the police (or other security agencies, like the Joint Military Task Force of the federal government) who were recently deployed in the Niger Delta to keep the peace.

Since this action is significantly responsible for the rate and intensity of youth restiveness in the Niger Delta, it is recommended that such sponsors of youth restiveness in the region should be identified and appropriately reprimanded and punished to discourage this tendency that is becoming popular among these unscrupulous leaders.

9.2.6 Electoral Reforms

One of the problems negatively affecting and compounding the emergence of Nigeria as a great democracy, with well-developed institutions and economy, had been the electoral process. In the past years of democracy in Nigeria, the country has been inundated with electoral malpractices that had always thrown up leaders who were not preferred by the electorates to lead them. Because of the paucity of the electoral process, corrupt and tainted leaders were foisted on the people, and for them to stay afloat, since they are swimming in the nation's oil wealth, they will always want to do everything possible to stay in power. To achieve this, they circumvent the already flawed electoral law to illegally perpetuate their terms in office. They, therefore, believe in hiring thugs and arming the already vulnerable youths to use them to foment trouble and chaos to scare away opponents preferred by the populace and electorates.

A good and robust electoral act will significantly minimize the hiccups inherent in the process of electing leaders in the country. Once credible leaders are put on board, it will reduce the rate at which unfit leaders are thrown upon the people. It will also reduce the tendency of having leaders who take delight in misusing youths for thuggery and other vices that breed youth restiveness in the Niger Delta.

In recognition of this, the federal government of Nigeria in 2008 instituted the Uwais Electoral Reform Commission to suggest ways that credible elections could be conducted so credible leaders could be chosen. The commission's report has already been adapted and put into action with the recent signing into law of the 2010 Electoral Act of the National Assembly by President Goodluck Jonathan. This law was used to conduct the 2011 elections in Nigeria. Although several flaws were noticed while implementing the adapted version of the Uwais Document, there is great lining of hope, as the 2011 elections were adjudged to be the first ever conclusively free elections held in Nigeria.

9.2.7 Eradicate Illegal Oil Bunkering

The monumental illegal oil bunkering activities ongoing in Niger Delta Region form a vast and booming business. Since it is a very big business, one needs huge capital to invest, given the risks involved. It is common knowledge that such capital needed to stay in illegal bunkering business cannot be afforded by the youths of these Niger Delta communities. There is every indication that such activities are carried out and sustained by very rich and well-endowed, but unscrupulous business elements that sponsor the youths to undertake the illegal operations that support this business. Without such enormous capital support, the youths will not be able to have enough to invest in this business.

Illegal Oil bunkering has, therefore, led to several vices that have befallen the Niger Delta Region in the peak of the region's crises, and even the post-peak period. Apart from negatively impacting the oil revenue profile and earnings of the federal government, it has created pockets of money, especially in the ranks of rogues and criminals who use such only for amassing weapons and facilitating restive conditions in the region.

The government should intensively search for and identify the sponsors of illegal bunkering activities in the region. Also, ships ferrying illegally bunkered oil should be stopped and their owners and crew arrested and properly prosecuted. There is also the need to seek and adopt technologies that can easily identify stolen oil, which is presently available in advanced economies. If these, among others, are not done, this very significant source of funding of restiveness in the Niger Delta Region will still remain fertile and robust.

9.2.8 Enhancing Corporate Social Responsibility in Oil-Producing Communities

Many oil-bearing Niger Delta communities who have oil installations and facilities from where the wealth of the nation is derived are very impoverished, lacking in infrastructure and basic amenities. In many cases, the communities have a dual economy, where squalor and poverty lay side by side the modem economy established by the multinational oil companies. The oil companies' facilities are always well lit, with good drinking water and internet facilities, among others. On the other hand, the communities that host their pride stay in slums characterized by darkness, poor housing infrastructure, poor sanitation, and an unreliable transportation network. In many of these communities, the people are restricted from having any access to the use of facilities of the multinational oil companies they host. These conditions, in many cases, breed discontent and are a significant reason that communities agitate for facilities. In many cases, as earlier noted in this text, such agitations have given rise to the restive situation in the Niger Delta Region.

Therefore, to eradicate restiveness arising from community agitations, government and the multinational oil companies should enhance their corporate social responsibilities in the communities. For these communities to regard the companies operating in the areas as their own, they must be seen to be benefiting from these neighbours. Access to basic amenities like good and safe drinking water, electricity, good housing, and affordable transportation should be extended by the companies and government to the communities. Also, the government should not abandon the communities to the multinational companies. The government should wake up to their responsibility to provide these basic amenities to the communities. Thus, if the oil companies come in to assist the government and communities in terms of projects, it should not be seen and regarded as their constitutional duty.

Overall, we opine that if corporate social responsibility is enhanced by the government and the oil companies, communities and most of their restive youths will find less room to make issues into a reason for restiveness.

9.2.9 Reduction of Arms Proliferation in the Niger Delta

It is common knowledge that the Niger Delta Region is replete with light and medium weapons. In some cases, sophisticated arms like surface-to-air missiles and rocket launchers have been discovered to be stored in the arsenals of the militant groups in the Niger Delta. A proof of this menacing acquisition and holding of arms by the Niger Delta youths was noticed during the Niger Delta amnesty program, where the armed youths were persuaded to return their arms and ammunitions for peace and other life-changing support. It has been strongly argued within and outside the Niger Delta Region—and even by the repentant militants themselves—that the weapons claimed to have been turned in by the militants represented a fraction of what they have in their stockpile. This, therefore, is an indication that there is still a preponderance of arms in the Niger Delta. Even after the convocation of amnesty in the region and the vows made by the militants to desist from their restive acts, there are still pockets of insurgencies (kidnapping, murders, armed robbery, among others) still being perpetuated by some splinter sections of the militants. The post-amnesty actions of Gen. Togo, a former repentant militant who went back to the trenches to refresh and continue restive militant activities, is a case to support our assertion here.

If lasting peace is to be obtained in the region, efforts must be put in place to further mop up arms from the restive youths. If government has done its own side of the agreement it signed with the militant youths, the youths must reciprocate by totally denouncing the arms struggle and truthfully turning in their remaining weapons and ammunitions. When the youths fail to perfect their own side of the agreement, after the government has totally committed, the government and its security agencies should isolate the criminals amongst the youths and deal with them as criminals, according to the laws of the land, while intensifying surveillance on their sponsors (who are mostly politicians and businessmen and women) to cut off their supply chain and contacts. It is also important for government and its security agencies to study and find out the other supply sources of arms into the region. Once the supply sources are crippled, even with a fixed demand, the price to acquire the product will be high, thus making the product dearer.

Figure 9.2: Rise in Price of Arms Due to Fall in Supply of Arms Given Fixed Demand

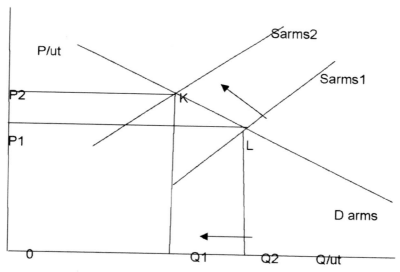

The diagram above shows the demand and supply of arms in the Niger Delta Region.

If supply management policies, aimed at contracting supply are put in place (supply depressing strategies), for instance, an outright closure of supply sources, the price of arms will increase from P1 to P2, given fixed demand for arms at D arms. This indicates that as price increases, the quantity demanded of arms will reduce. The movement of price from P1 to P2 creates a new equilibrium with the constant demand function D arms at K. Thus, increasing price of arms from P1 to P2 and reducing quantity effectively demanded from the market from Q2 to Q1.

In practice, supply-depressing policies will be more effective than demand-depressing policies to correct this arms market, by making supply of unwanted goods and products unavailable. Even when parallel market are created, the effective price in the illegal market will always be higher than the price in the legal market, considering the risk factor of having to contravene government supply restraining policy on arms that will definitely impact the parallel market prices upwards.

Specifically, illegal supply of arms and ammunitions into the Niger Delta Region, for example the ones indicated to be supplied into the market from the illegal supply corridors of the militant youths, should be targeted and curtailed or totally stopped. Also, proper monitoring and search of vessels, especially in the oil sector, that enter into our territorial waters should be intensified.

9.2.10 Proper Manning of the Country's Borders

The country's naval and immigration services have openly confessed that the nation's boundaries are porous and will therefore require more intensive monitoring. For such a confession to come from agencies that the country's hope relies on for protection from external aggressors, then the situation is grim and needs an emergency kind of treatment from the government. If the borders of the country are properly manned, it will reduce incidences of arms being smuggled into the country and more specifically, the Niger Delta Region. In order to attain the goal of proper manning of our country's porous borders, it is important that we eliminate or reduce significantly the incidence of corruption in the country's total economic, social and political structure.

Another injurious report in the country is that legal arms imported into the country and meant for the security agencies are now found in the custody of people who are not duly authorized to hold such arms. There have been reported cases where arms and ammunitions meant for the police and even the army is sold to criminals who are not entitled to use such weapons. This situation is caused by corrupt people in the system. Recently, a divisional police officer was arrested in Enugu State as the main mastermind of kidnapping and other criminal activities in the state. Notably, Enugu State is a state close to the states of the Niger Delta but in the South East region of Nigeria (Vanguard Newspaper, 16th March 2011). This and many others similar cases show a near total systemic decay that has encouraged and thrown up scenarios where security agents have become agents of social destruction.

9.2.11 Creation of Employment Opportunities

Unemployment has been confirmed to be very high, especially among the employable group, in Nigeria. In explaining the Niger Delta crises over the years, many analysts, groups and commentators who have had work to do with and in the Niger Delta Region have singled out unemployment as one of the main causes of youth restiveness in the region. These youths stay unemployed and earning no income, giving them and their stored-up energies freedom to engage in whatever they see to make a living. In many cases, such openings are more in vices and illegal activities. The argument in many cases has been that these youths are unemployable since they do not possess the requisite skills for employment in the nearby oil companies and their subsidiaries. Also, employment in government is far from these youths; the government seems to have abdicated its responsibilities to the oil companies operating in the region. The people thus see and regard the oil companies as the ones that should provide their basic necessities of life: education, health, and employment, among others.

Since unemployment has been identified as a key instigator of youth restiveness in the Niger Delta, government should start creating jobs for the teeming youths. Apart from creating jobs itself, government should create an enabling environment to encourage self-employment opportunities, such as provisions of affordable credit through government guarantees, tax holidays, and other enticing incentives. There are many youths in the region who are well trained in some arts and vocations like hairdressing, barbering, welding, and ICT, among others. Their training for this expertise is mostly provided and anchored by oil companies, NGOs, and sometimes government. Regrettably, these trained youths do not have power (electricity) and complementary infrastructure that would have helped them establish and run their trade.

9.2.12 Isolating Criminals from the Niger Delta Liberation Struggle

The Niger Delta struggle has come up with several outcomes, some of which include pockets of criminality adorning and garnishing the Niger Delta liberation struggle. Criminals have usurped the opportunity of the genuine struggles to infringe mayhem in the region through involvement in criminal activities like armed robbery, kidnapping, burglary, outright assassinations, raping, among others. The echoes or after effect of the cessation of hostilities by genuine agitators in the Niger Delta have been the pockets of violent crimes being perpetuated by the criminal content of the true liberation fighters. There is therefore the need for actions to isolate the criminals from the true agitators.

Continuous perpetuation of kidnapping, armed robbery, rapes, etc. in the region after the amnesty exposes the true and obvious criminal content of the liberation struggle. If the government can therefore carefully and painstakingly isolate the criminals from the real agitators for liberation of the Niger Delta Region, it will be able to treat criminals in the way they should be treated, with relevant laws of the land that deals with such issues, while going on with its planned amnesty program, which is designed to reform the true Niger Delta militants.

9.2.13 Moral and Ethical Re-orientation of Criminal Activities Enablers

A careful participatory study and analysis of the Niger Delta militancy exposes the inert and unexposed aspect of some traditional psychological and philosophical enablers that emboldens the militants and even criminal elements in the Niger Delta Region to entrench their activities (the vices).

The role and activities of local witchdoctors and traditional medicine practitioners and providers must be located and analyzed. Many of the militants and criminals studied in the region emphasize clearly that they visit to get psychic powers that repel bullets and even insulate them from acid baths and intense beatings if they are caught eventually. They also receive predictions of what will happen in the future or following their criminal events. In many cases, the spiritual psychic power providers even advertise these powers. One thing that comes out of this is that spiritual power providers give some real level of confidence and psychological buffer to these criminals and militants. With this false idea of being totally secure from any attack (bullet, acid, etc.), they go into their criminal activities with impunity.

9.2.14 Eschewing Criminal Persecution of Political Opponents

It is becoming very common in the Niger Delta Region, the use of criminal persecution as a tool to cow and bury opponents. The governments here are very intolerant and will not want to see any opposition. Any criticism of their activities is seen and considered as criminal and such critics must be so treated. The resultant eclipse of opposition and the alternate view, makes the government become docile and passive, with real hyping of "praise singers" and sycophants (a common feature in Nigeria), bereft of the real needs of the people and how the people perceive and genuinely accept their projects and programs outside the confines of intimidation.

9.2.15 Developing A Model for Early Identification of Similar Spots in the Country

It should be noted that youth restiveness in the Niger Delta and, in fact, Nigeria cannot be said to be an item that was imported from outside the country. The situation and conditions prevalent for its emergence and sustenance brewed within the communities, and as such, there are various indicators that one could have immediately described the character of the output (youth restiveness). Such indicators abound elsewhere, even in pockets, all over the country. For instance, kidnapping that was used as a warfare tool by the Niger Delta militants to intimidate foreign oil workers in order to attract international attention eventually permeated to its neighbouring South Eastern region states, where the youths there brazenly and menacingly substituted it (kidnapping) for armed robbery and advanced fee fraud to make illegal money from its citizens. Kidnapping has become terribly bad and embarrassing now in the South East region. Here, the youths are involved in kidnapping for money and not for any ideological reason like in the Niger Delta where it is a tool in the basket of tools used for the region's liberation struggle. There are trends that this criminal tendency may spread like a virus to all other regions of the country not experiencing it now if it is not cut and terminated at the bud. Resulting from this argument, therefore, it is recommended that the government of the Federal Republic of Nigeria should evolve mechanisms that could be used for early identification of similar spots in the country that could be "youth-restive compliant," given the identification of restiveness enabling condition-prevalent situation. Such knowledge will help in building a model that can guarantee prior identification of spots where youth restiveness will thrive in the country once those enabling conditions are found.

BIBLIOGRAPHY

Ashton-Jones, N., Arnott, S. & Douglas, 0. (1998). *The Human Ecosystems of the Niger Delta*. Benin City: Environmental Rights Action (EPA).

Ashton-Jones, N., Arnott, S. & Douglas, O. (1998). The ERA Handbook.

Alagoa, E. J (1999). *The land and People of Bayelsa State: Central Niger Delta*. Port Harcourt: Onyoma Research Publications.

Aderinokun, K. (2007, 9th July). Oil Revenue Drops by N262bn. ThisDay Newspaper.

Aderinokun. K. (2007, July 14th). Insecurity Stalls N2GGbn Project in the Niger Delta. Punch Newspapers.

Amnesty International (2006), Nigeria: Oil, Poverty and Violence.

Andrew, R., Green, B., & Routledge, (1996). A Shell-shocked land for details of Royal Dutch Shell's activities in Uniuechern in the central Niger Delta. London.

Abdoulaye Ndiaye, Conservation and Sustainable Development Strategy for the Niger Delta." The John D. and Catharine T. Mac Arthur Foundation (mimeo) pp. 5-6.

Ake, C. (1996). *Democracy and Development*. Washington DC: Brooking Institution.

Bannet and Okurptifa (1984).

Boahen, A. (1966). *Topics in West African History*. London: Longman.

Bob, S. (2007). Postscript to the Article: World inequality and globalization. *Oxford Review of Economic Policy*, Spring 2004.

Blomquist, N. (1981). A Comparison of Distributions of Annual and Lifetime Income: Sweden around 1970. A Review of Income and wealth, 27 (3), 243-264.

British Broadcasting Corporation (2009, May 21). www. bbcnews.com.

Carter, P. (2007). United States Department of State. Remarks on US and international Cooperation in the Niger River Delta.

Country Analysis, Nigeria- (2003) and Central Intelligence Agency (CIA) reported in Saipem (2004) and the World Fact Book. Nigeria (2003).

Carreyrou, J. (2005, November; A1, A15). Culture Clash, Muslim groups may gain strength from French Unrest. *The Wall Street Journal*, 246 (83).

Cross River State Broadcasting Service (2004). CBSnews. com.

David, K. (1994, April). The Coming Anarchy. *Atlantic Monthly*.

Deutsch, J. S. Hakim, and Spiegel, U. (1990). Learning by Criming: Theoretical Analysis and Empirical Evidence. *Public Finance, 45* (1), 59-69.

DiPasquale, D & Glazer, E. L. (1998). The Los Angeles Riot and the Economics of Urban Unrest. *Journal of Urban Economics, 43* (1), 52-78.

Edwards, M. E. (2007). *Regional and Urban Economic and Economic Development*. New York: Auerbach Publications-Taylor & Francis Group.

Ekong, C. N. & Ayara, N. N. (2002). The Gains and Strength in Participation: A case Study of Mbiabet Ikpe Rice Farm Project in Nigeria. *International Institute for Environment and Development,* (44), 60-64.

Ekong, C. N. (2008). Community Savings and Credit Scheme: A Guide. Nigeria: Piotoru Books. Port Harcourt.

Ekong, C. N. (2008). Study on the Root Causes of Youth Restiveness in the Niger Delta Region. Commissioned by Uyo Conscience-a Socio-political group in the Niger Delta Region.

Ekong, C. N., & Onye, K. U. (2012). Economic Development in Nigeria: The Basic Needs Approach. *Journal of Economics and Sustainable Development,* 3 (10), 54-65.

Environmental Resources Management Ltd. (1997). Niger Delta Environmental Survey final report Phase 1: Volume 1.

Firebaugh, G. (1999). Empirics of World Income Inequality. *American Journal of Sociology,* 104 (6), 1597 – 1630, Doi: 10:1086/210218.

Firebaugh, G. (2003). Inequality: What and how it is measured-The New Geography of Global Income Inequality. Cambridge MA: Harvard Univ. Press.

Human Rights Watch (1999). The Price of Oil: Corporate Responsibility and Human Rights Violations in Nigeria's Oil Producing Communities.

Iyoha, P.C., Oviasunji, P. O, Ojo, S.O. (2003). Women, Youth Restiveness and Development in the Niger Delta. Benin: Ambrose Alli, University Institute of Governance & Development.

Imobigha, T. A., Bassey, C. O., & Asini, J. B. (2002). *Conflict and Instability in the Niger Delta: the Warri Case.* Ibadan: Spectrum Books Ltd.

Khan, A. S. (1994). *The Political Economy of Oil.* USA: Oxford University Press.

Koragiannis, E & Koraceric, M. (2000). A method to calculate the Jacknife Variance Estimator for the Gini Coefficient. *Oxford Bulletin of Economics and Statistic,* 62, 119-122.

Madunagu, E. (2007, July 14th). Insecurity stalls N266bn Projects in the Niger Delta. Punch Newspaper.

McLennan, J.; Stewart, W. (Feb, 2005). Deepwater Africa reaches turning point. Oil and Gas Journal. Vol. 103, 6; ABI/INFORM Global. Pg. 18.

Milner, J. R. (1987). Politics, work and daily life in the USSR, New York: Cambridge Univ. p. 193. ISBN 0521348900.

Nigeria Business Info.com, (2008).

Natural Gas. Online Nigeria (2008).

Nigeria Liquefied Natural Gas Ltd (LNG) (1997). From Nigeria: London NNPC and Academic Associates Peaceworks (2008), Report of the Niger Delta Youth Stakeholders Workshop, PHC, April 15–16, 2008, pp. 48 and 51.

Overseas Security Advisory Council (2008)—Crime & Safety Report—CRIME & SAFETY—Global Security News (OSAC)—Sub Saharan Africa—Nigeria, 29 April.

Obi, C. (2006). Youth and the Generational Dimension to struggles for Resources Control in the Niger Delta: Prospects for the Nation—State Project in Nigeria. The CODESRIA Monograph Series.

Ogoni Bill of Rights, (1992), Saros International Publishers, Port Harcourt, Nigeria.

Okonta, I. and Oronto Douglas, (1998), "Where Vultures Feast: Forty Years of Shell in the Niger Delta", Sierra Club Books/Random, New York, forthcoming. See particularly chapter six, "Ambush in the Night."

Ogwang, T. (2000). A Convenient method of computing the Gini Index and its standard Error", Oxford Bulletin of Economics and Statistics 62:123–129 Results: Reply. Oxford Bulletin of Economics and Statistics 66:435–437.

Ogwang, Tomson (2004). Calculating Standard Error for the Gini Coefficient: some further.

Okechukwu, I. (2008). (ed) Oiling Violence: the Proliferation of Illegal Arms and Light Weapons in the Niger Delta: Abuja; Frederick Elberstifting.

Okechukwu, I. & Ike, I. (2006). Antinomies of Wealth: Oil Revenue, Allocation, Distribution and Utilization in the Niger Delta: A Research Report submitted to Oxford GB, Abuja.

Okechukwu, I. (2004). The Rhetoric of Right: Understanding the Changing Discourse of Rights in the Niger Delta; ACAS Bulletin.

Overseas Security Advisory Council (OSAC)–Global Security News (2008, 29th April). Crime and Safety Report–CRIME & SAFETY sub Saharan Africa–Nigeria.

Poling, J. (2003, April 8). Country Responsibilities in Achieving the Millennium Development Goals. Washington DC.

Project Underground Human Rights and Environmental Information on the Royal Dutch/Shell Group of companies 1996 – 1997, Berkeley, California, April 1997, p.15.

Ray, D. (1988). *Development Economics*. Princeton University Press. ISBN 0691017069.

Robert, L. and Okechukwu, I. (2002). Nigeria: Military Rule, Democratization, Conflict and Corporate Responsibility in a Petro-state. Discussion Paper for the Meeting on "Oil and Conflict," Bellagio, Italy, Nov. 18-22.

Shell International Petroleum Company, Developments in Nigeria (1995, March). London.

Sunday Times, London, "Shell axes corrupt Nigeria staff,' 17 December, 1995.

Terry K. (1997). Paradox of Plenty. Berkely, California: University of California Press.

The ERA Handbook to the Niger Delta (1998). Benin.

This Day Newspaper (2007, 16th July). Plans to Arrest Youth Restiveness in Niger Delta.

This day Newspaper (2007. 9th July).

The Guardian Editorial (2007, 17th July). Kidnapping of Children.

ThisDay Newspaper (2000, 9th May).

Transparency Initiative (2009), "Annual Report."

UNDP (2008), "Country Report, MDG."

United States *Energy Information Administration* (US EIA) (1997, December). Nigeria Country Analysis Brief.

Niger Delta Human Development Report: Ways to Enhance Security in the Niger Delta. www.vanqaurdngr.com.

Vanguard Newspaper (2007, July 17).

www.nigrianoil-gas.com/ and www.nipc-nigeria.org/

Federal Bureau of Statistics (2009) p. 107.

Environmental Rights Action (2008).

Vanguard Newspaper, 16th March, 2011.

Lightning Source UK Ltd.
Milton Keynes UK
UKOW02f0322070317
295975UK00002B/550/P